COMPANIONS TO CLEMATIS

COMPANIONS TO CLEMATIS

MARIGOLD BADCOCK

First published 2000 by
Guild of Master Craftsman Publications Ltd,
166 High Street, Lewes,
East Sussex BN7 1XU

Reprinted 2000

ISBN 1 86108 151 0

A catalogue record of this book is available from
the British Library.

Editors: Andy Charman & Nicola Wright
Designer: Joyce Chester
Cover designer: Ian Smith
Illustrator (line drawings): John Yates
Typefaces: Sabon, Frutiger and Lithos
Colour origination by Viscan Graphics P.L., Singapore
Printed and bound by Kyodo Printing (Singapore) under the
supervision of MRM Graphics, Winslow, Buckinghamshire, UK

10 9 8 7 6 5 4 3 2 1

CONTENTS

INTRODUCTION
page 1

1 THE CLEMATIS GROUPS
page 6

2 CULTIVATION
page 66

3 PARTNERS FOR SPRING
page 88

4 SUMMER SPLENDOUR
page 116

5 AUTUMN GLORY
page 144

Glossary *page 162*

About the Author *page 164*

Useful Addresses *page 165*

Index *page 166*

ACKNOWLEDGEMENTS

TO family and friends who gave their help and encouragement and to neighbours who so kindly allowed me to photograph their clematis, I offer my sincere thanks; this book would not have been possible without you.

I would also like to thank the many people and organizations who have allowed photographs to be taken for this book, including the following:

Those gardeners in the south-west and south-east of England who open their gardens in aid of charity; the magnificence of your plants was surpassed only by the hospitality you extended.

The British Clematis Society and their exciting collection at the national display garden Bourne Hall, Ewell, Surrey; The Royal Horticulture Society, Wisley and Rosemoor; Eggesford Garden Centre, Devon; Rode Bird Garden, Somerset; Royal National Rose Society, St. Albans.

Special thanks to Dr Jimmy Smart and his team at Marwood Hill Gardens, Devon. These beautiful gardens were a constant source of inspiration and your help was truly appreciated.

Personal thanks to Andy Charman at GMC Publications for his help on my first venture into writing. To Sheila Lovell, for the beautiful watercolour illustrations.

And finally, to Edward who was there every step of the way; this book is dedicated to you.

INTRODUCTION

I WAS first introduced to clematis many years ago when visiting a small nursery in Berkshire. I was looking for a climber to grow over a large, unsightly shed with a roof of corrugated tin. A friend had suggested an evergreen honeysuckle, the nurseryman recommended a *montana* clematis; I bought both, planting one each end of the shed in small pockets of earth that had been left in the concrete surrounds. I have always been a great believer in bonemeal, so they probably had a handful each and were left to get on with it. And get on with it they did; within three years the shed was virtually covered and the battle had begun to decide which one could outdo the other. We moved

A rose and a clematis tumbling freely over a pergola

A pink *montana*, a rampant climber, scales a roof that has been covered with wire netting

house before either gave way and I sometimes wonder what happened to them. Did they carry on over the back of the shed into the adjacent garden and clamber over everything in their path? Or did one finally take over and smother the other? If so, which one? My bet would be on the *montana* to win.

Although I was fond of the honeysuckle, it was the mass of pink *montana* blooms in May that excited me and led me to seek other clematis for the garden. Soon the fences were covered in a variety of different clematis, each one with its own defined space. I knew little about the variety of species, cultivars and hybrids at the time; I just bought something

C. 'Jackmanii' produces masses of purple blooms

'Jackmanii Alba', a hybrid of 'Jackmanii x fortunei', has single blooms as the season progresses

if I liked the colour or shape of the flower, pruning it in accordance with the instructions on the label and in order to keep it confined. 'Jackmanii' refused to be confined and became entwined with my favourite climbing rose 'Compassion'; the mass of large purple heads with the salmon-pink rose was simply stunning and gave me insight into the wonderful potential of clematis to enhance other plants. Imagine my disappointment when one day, out of the blue, 'Jackmanii' drooped and died. Instinctively I cut it down and nearly dug it up in case the disease (unknown to me at the time) should infect my beloved rose. I decided to take a chance. It had its reprieve and was fed and watered along with 'Compassion'. To my delight 'Jackmanii' was soon shooting new stems and the next season the mass of purple blooms was even more prolific.

Clematis like 'Lady Northcliffe' make ideal companions for roses

After this scare, I read all that I could about clematis and discovered that the problem could have been clematis wilt. I visited a specialist clematis grower in Hertfordshire from whom I learnt to plant clematis deeply in enriched soil and to insert a feeding tube at the time of planting to enable water and food to reach the roots more easily. I can remember his advice to this day: 'Once a week, during the growing season, fill up your watering can, adding the correct amount of potash-based fertilizer, and pour it down the feeding tube until it overflows.' My husband and I did this conscientiously and our clematis grew stronger, healthier and more beautiful each year. I learnt to prune in accordance with their type, but now gave them their freedom to tumble over shrubs and plants just as they pleased. Our small garden became a picture of colour throughout the seasons.

I have not always been patient enough to follow the other sound advice given by the specialist nurseryman: 'to hard prune all clematis, regardless of type, at the time of planting and to continue to hard prune until six stems emerge from the base'. With late-flowering varieties this is fine, because the flowers are formed on the current year's growth, but the early varieties bloom on the previous years' growth and it seems such a long wait for the flowers. These days I tend to compromise by hard pruning in the first February after planting – this usually encourages at least one other stem to form – and from then on, with the early-flowering varieties, I hard prune every other stem until a healthy number are growing from the base. This satisfies my need to have flowers early in the season and the clematis' need to put energy into stem production.

I love gardens where plants intermingle, weaving through borders like threads in a tapestry and in my opinion, just as hills and mountains add grandeur to a landscape, so trees, shrubs and climbers add height and variation to the garden. We have always had modest-sized gardens where only the small varieties of trees could be accommodated and this encouraged me to seek height in other ways. I planted clematis and other climbers on poles and pergolas; clematis clambered over shrubs where their bright colours drew the eye upward, and the house walls were covered with roses and wisteria, enabling clematis to tumble through them. My husband used to jest that if you stood still long enough in our garden you would soon be covered with clematis.

Two years ago, just as the garden was maturing, the opportunity arose for us to move to the West Country where we now face

'Rouge Cardinal', a late-flowering hybrid, looks wonderful alone or growing through golden leaves

the wonderful challenge of creating a cottage garden to surround our lovely old cob cottage. When we started to design the garden and to think of planting schemes, I referred to the notes I had kept on ideas for planting clematis with host plants. It occurred to me how useful it would be to have a list of clematis by season, colour and height to help me to select clematis to grow through existing shrubs and to plan combinations to enhance many aspects of the garden throughout the year. From this idea grew the inspiration to write this book.

The first chapter is devoted to presenting the various groups of clematis, eleven in total, with a brief description of colour, features and height. I hope that this fairly comprehensive list will help you to choose just the right clematis for specific locations in your garden.

No book on clematis would be complete without a discussion of the various methods and ideas for planting and caring for these plants. Unfortunately, clematis still struggle with the reputation of being difficult to grow and I suppose it is not totally undeserved, because they do need a fair amount of tender

Clematis 'Caroline' and *Rosa* 'Mme Isaac Pereire'

loving care, especially regular watering, if they are to flourish. I still occasionally have a young clematis droop with wilt and I do what I did instinctively with 'Jackmanii': cut it down, give it water and food and hope for the best. Invariably I am rewarded. I have learnt that there are many types of clematis that appear to be disease resistant, especially amongst the smaller-flowered varieties. Keep at bay the few pests and diseases to which a clematis is susceptible and once it has become established in a spot where it is happy, you will have a loyal friend for many years.

I hope that by sharing some of my ideas for planting clematis with host plants in spring, summer and autumn that you will feel inspired to create your own special combinations, perhaps by using some of the shrubs, climbers, trees and structures already established in your own garden.

Photography has become an absorbing hobby for me, and I especially enjoy trying to capture the beauty of flowers. During the past year I have looked closely through the lens at hundreds of different clematis and have become greatly intrigued by the intricacy of their stamen, pistil and sepal formations and their wonderful combinations of colours. I have discovered that the colour of a clematis is affected by its location. For example, a pink 'Hagley Hybrid' planted in full sun is often a very faded specimen compared to one that grows in shade.

I have endeavoured to capture clematis as they appear in their true environment, a mission that was challenged by the weather. On grey days with heavy cloud there is usually insufficient light to use the slow 50 ASA film that captures the vibrancy of colour so successfully. Conversely, bright sunlight washes out the colours. Despite the excellent quality of the modern day camera lens and the capability of colour film to portray glorious

'Hagley Hybrid' should be grown in semi-shade to protect the delicate colour from fading

images, neither can reproduce the subtlety of colour and tone experienced by the human eye. For example, it is a well-known fact that blue flowers are difficult to photograph as they often portray a purple or pink tone. Please bear this in mind when looking at photographs of Clematis 'Perle d'Azur', 'Multi Blue' and others described as blue toned, the human eye really does see them differently. The worst enemy of the photographer, however, is wind; even the slightest breeze moves these delicate flowers, making it difficult to capture that fraction of a second when the flower is still. I can recall only a few days in the year that I have been taking these pictures when conditions were really good for photography, but I hope that the resulting photographs will give an indication of the beauty these flowers can bring to your garden.

In *Companions to Clematis* I have tried to provide information for gardeners who are seeking to plant clematis for the first time and for those who may wish to increase their collection. I hope that it will inspire you to try many different planting combinations and, as your ideas continue to grow, that you will feel as I do: that there is always room for just one more clematis.

THE CLEMATIS
GROUPS

Clematis 'Special Occasion' a mid-season large-flowered cultivar

THERE are over 250 known species of clematis, originating from both hemispheres. Many of these species were found growing in remote and wild regions and we can thank the botanist explorers of the past few centuries for the wonderful range and variety of clematis that are now available.

Whilst admiring the bravery of these adventurers, we must also recognize the valuable role played by amateur and professional clematis breeders internationally, who, with great skill and a little luck, have cross-bred the species and produced so many beautiful cultivars and hybrids. The excitement remains today, with specialist growers and keen amateur gardeners striving to produce new and unusual plants.

With such a wide choice of clematis available and with new varieties appearing on the market each year, it is virtually impossible to present a fully comprehensive list. This chapter is devoted to submitting as many species, hybrids and cultivars as possible to enable the reader to select clematis by season, colour, form and habit to suit his or her particular gardening needs. Finding new or different alternatives from your suppliers can be part of the fun of becoming a clematis collector.

Structure, habit and shape

Clematis is a member of the Ranunculaceae (buttercup) family and the name is derived from the Greek word *klema* meaning 'vine branch'. You may have heard it pronounced in a couple of ways. Evidently the correct pronunciation is Klem-a-tis with the 'a' as in apple and without emphasis. In other words, it is not 'Klem-aye-tis' but 'Klematis'. This is not an important point, because it is a beautiful genus of plants whichever way you say it, but it may be a little mystery solved for some readers.

Throughout the book you will come across the terms 'species', 'hybrids' and 'cultivars'. 'Species' indicates that the flowers and foliage are of the plant's original habit. If several species of one genus are cultivated together they may 'hybridize', creating offspring that could be similar to their parents or bear no resemblance. A cultivar, however, is artificially raised and its characteristics can be maintained by propagation.

Clematis flowers appear in a variety of shapes and sizes from 1 to 2cm (½ to ¾in) up to 20cm (8in) across, or more.

The colour and formation of the stamens play an important role and it is often this feature that individualizes flowers of a similar structure and hue.

We are perhaps becoming a bit too technical when we state that clematis do not actually form petals (the corolla). The flowers are made by the sepals (the calyx) alone. On a rose we can see the combination of coloured petals and green sepals beneath. The sepals protect

Clematis are valued not only for their colours but also for the wide variety of flower shapes they offer

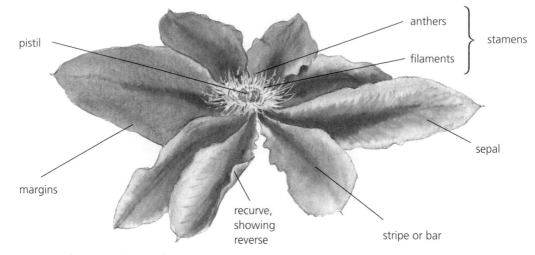

The various parts of a typical clematis flower

the bud and fold back as the flower opens to reveal the whorl of coloured petals. Clematis have a circle of sepals which, instead of being green, have developed into lovely colours and to all intents and purposes look just like petals.

To complicate matters even more, we often

Clematis cling to supports with their coiling tendrils

see clematis petals referred to as 'tepals'. This can only be very simply explained by the fact that in many genus of flowers the sepal and petals are identical and they both whorl around together; they are then collectively known as tepals. It is natural therefore that clematis petals could be referred to in this way. In this text they have been referred to as sepals, in order to provide continuity. This is a mere technicality, because whether we call them petals or sepals, they look like petals and that is how we tend to think of them.

Clematis that climb can only do so with the aid of a structure or host plant. As part of their leaf construction, they develop coiling tendrils that curl around any suitable means of support in their pathway.

In the wild, clematis naturally clamber over hedges and bushes and often climb high into trees. *C. vitalba*, the native clematis of Britain, often called old man's beard because of its fluffy seed heads, is a well-known sight at the edge of woods and forests and in hedgerows, where it makes a charming companion to the wild rose, particularly in autumn when the seed heads and orange rose hips are produced in abundance. Much can be learnt by observing the growth and habit of wild

C. alpina 'Frances Rivis' blooms in spring and as a category 1 variety does not need to be pruned

clematis: they naturally plant their feet in the shade and climb vigorously over a host plant or tree to have their heads in the sun. This natural habit is what we will try to emulate in some of the examples and ideas for garden planting shown in following chapters.

The herbaceous clematis group does not have coiling tendrils and they can only scramble around and over other plants. Some varieties, however, will climb to 2m (6½ft) if given support.

For cultivation purposes, clematis are presented in three categories (see panel).

THE THREE CATEGORIES OF CLEMATIS

Category 1 – *cirrhosa*, *armandii*, *alpina*, *macropetala* and *montana*. These varieties bloom in winter, spring and early summer, depending upon the type, and do not need to be pruned.

Category 2 – early/mid-season, large-flowered varieties which bloom in the late spring and early summer and require light pruning only.

Category 3 – *viticella*; *texensis*; *orientalis*; herbaceous; late, large-flowered; and late, small-flowered varieties which bloom from summer to autumn, most of which require hard pruning.

THE EVERGREEN CLIMBERS
C. CIRRHOSA AND C. ARMANDII

Flowering season: *cirrhosa*: November–March; *armandii*: March–April

Flowers: *cirrhosa*: open, bell-shaped flowers and attractive seed heads; *armandii*: saucer-shaped flowers

Aspect: Warm, sunny wall in mild-climate zone. Alternatively, conservatory or sheltered porch. Rampant growth; allow plenty of space

Cultivation: Follow recommended planting and feeding programme

Pruning: Category 1. None required, because flowers are formed on previous year's growth. If necessary, prune lightly after flowering to contain growth

Background: *Clematis cirrhosa* was introduced from southern Europe during the latter part of the sixteenth century. *Clematis armandii* was introduced from southern China in the early part of the twentieth century. Some interesting varieties have been bred from both species. The attractive evergreen foliage provides interest all year

A joy to behold in the midst of winter: the beautiful, delicate-scented flowers of the *cirrhosa* family need a warm, sheltered location

Variety	Colour	Features	Height (approx.)
C. cirrhosa	Cream, lightly speckled red inside	Fern-like foliage, bronze coloured in winter. Attractive seed heads. Citrus scent	4m (13ft)
var. *balaerica*	Deep cream with maroon spots inside	Slightly broader leaves, finely cut. Pointed sepals	4m (13ft)
'Calycina'	Cream, speckled as species	Open cup-shaped flowers born singly or in clusters. Broader, light bronze leaves. Attractive seed heads	4m (13ft)
'Early Sensation'	White with soft yellow stamens	Attractive green foliage. Prefers south-west aspect, sheltered	4m (13ft)
'Freckles'	Cream with grey tinge. Heavily speckled wine-red	Leaves larger than species	4.5m (15ft)
indivisa	White	A mass of daisy-like flowers. Small leaves	4.5m (15ft)
'Jingle Bells'	Cream buds opening to pure white flowers	Attractive dark green foliage	5m (16½ft)

Evergreen 'Early Sensation' lives up to its name as it decorates a wire-netting fence

Clematis cirrhosa 'Freckles' bears cream flowers tinged in grey with wine-red speckles

▲ Evergreen *indivisa* growing beautifully on a house wall in south-west England may not fare as well in a cooler part of the country

▶ *C. cirrhosa* 'Wisley Cream' needs a warm, sheltered wall or a conservatory. It can flower from November to March

Variety	Colour	Features	Height (approx.)
'Wisley Cream'	Cream with green tinge	Slightly broader leaves	4.5m (15ft)
✓ *armandii*	Creamy-white	Large, glossy leaves all year. Sweetly scented	6m (19½ft)
'Apple Blossom'	Pale pink buds opening to very pale	Rounded foliage tinged bronze. Apple-blossom fragrance	6m (19½ft)
'Bowl of Beauty'	White, bowl-shaped. Large clusters	Dark foliage	6m (19½ft)
'Meyeniana'	Cream with rose-pink flush	Large foliage, sweet scent. A very rare form introduced from Hong Kong	4.5m (15ft)
'Snowdrift'	Waxy-white	Heavily scented. Glossy green leaves all year	4.5m (15ft)

OTHER EVERGREENS

Variety	Colour	Features	Height (approx.)
'Joe' ('*Cartmanii* Joe')	White	Finely cut evergreen foliage. Flowers in profusion, April. Scrambling habit suited to rockery. Needs winter protection	Compact, rockery
forsteri	Creamy-white with a tinge of green; yellowish stamens	Scented flowers produced in profusion late spring/early summer	3–4m (10–13ft)
napaulensis	Creamy-white with long, deep red stamens	Flowers December–February. Semi-evergreen; leaves fall late summer, new leaves in winter	3–4m (10–13ft)
'Nunn's Gift'	Pale cream with green-yellow stamens	Twisted, veined sepals, March–April; Finely cut dark green foliage. Ideal for pot culture. Needs winter protection. New variety	Compact, rockery

The flowers of *Clematis forsteri* are about 4cm (1½in) across and grow in clusters

C. ALPINA

Flowering season: April–May, with some varieties having second flush in summer

Flowers: 2–5cm (¾–2in) single, open, bell shaped

Aspect: Any. Looks best when allowed to roam freely

Cultivation: Hardy, follow recommended planting and feeding programme. Do not disturb roots when planting

Pruning: Category 1. Tidy only, because flowers are formed on previous year's growth. If necessary, prune lightly after flowering to contain growth. Severe pruning should be avoided when the plant is mature

Background: *Alpina* species was introduced from mainland Europe at the end of the eighteenth century. Like *macropetala*, it is part of the Atragene group. There are a few selections of the species and a number of hybrids have been raised

C. alpina 'Pink Flamingo'

Variety	Colour	Features	Height (approx.)
alpina	Mid-blue with white stamens	Satin-like appearance	2–3m (6½–10ft) (applies to all varieties)
'Ametistina'	Mauve-red flushed pink	Occasional summer flowers	
'Betina'	Very deep brown-red	Recursive sepal	
'Bluebird'	Pale-blue	Large, frilly flowers	
'Blue Dancer'	Silver-blue	Slightly twisted sepals	
'Blush Queen'	Strong pink with fading margins	Large-flowered, boldly presented	
'Brunette'	Reddish-brown	Satin-like appearance. Occasional summer flowers	
'Burford White'	White		
alpina 'Columbine'	Pale-blue		
'Constance'	Pink-red	Semi-double. Occasional summer flowers	
'Cyanea'	Bright violet-blue	Profusion of flowers	
'Foxy'	Delicate pink with deeper pink centre	Occasional summer flowers	
'Frances Rivis'	Sky-blue	Lantern-shaped flowers	
'Frankie'	Mid-blue with white stamens tipped in matching blue		
'Helsingborg'	Deep purple-blue with darker stamens	Hybrid of *C. ochotensis* x *C. alpina*	
'Jacqueline du Pré'	Rosy-mauve edged in silvery pink	Stunning variety	
alpina 'Odorata'	Mid-blue	Sweetly scented	
'Pamela Jackman'	Deep blue	Profusion of flowers	
'Pauline'	Bright blue	Large flowers	
'Pink Flamingo'	Pale pink veined darker pink	Occasional summer flowers	
'Prairie River'	Violet-blue fading to white at the base of each sepal	Broad sepals	

C. alpina 'Frances Rivis'   C. alpina 'Ruby'

Variety	Colour	Features	Height (approx.)
alpina 'Rosy Pagoda'	Pink with white edges	Flowers in profusion	2–3m (6½–10ft) (applies to all varieties)
'Ruby'	Rosy-red with off-white stamens	Occasional summer flowers	
'Tage Lundell'	Mauve with pink stamens	Petal-shaped stamens	
'White Columbine'	Pure white	Long, tapering sepals. Profusion of flowers	
'White Moth'	White	Small, double flowers. Compact plant	
alpina 'Willy'	Pale pink with red base		

C. MACROPETALA

Flowering season: April–May with occasional second flush summer–early autumn

Flowers: 5–12cm (2–4¾in) Double in appearance, followed by attractive silver seed heads

Aspect: Any. Very hardy variety. Can grow 2–5m (6½–16½ft) even on a north-facing wall. Like *alpina* and *montana* this group is best left to roam with a natural look

Cultivation: Follow recommended planting and feeding programme. Take care not to disturb the roots when planting

Pruning: Category 1. None required, because flowers are formed on previous year's growth. If necessary, prune lightly after flowering to contain growth. Severe pruning should be avoided, especially when the plant is fully mature

Background: *C. macropetala* species was introduced from China during the early nineteeth century. The original species is still one of the finest with its lavender-blue flowers tinged mauve at the edge

C. macropetala is a hardy species that can withstand the wintery conditions of a cold spring

Variety	Colour	Features	Height (approx.)
C. macropetala	Lavender-blue, tinged mauve	Sepals have a felt-like texture	2–2.5m (6½–8ft) (applies to all varieties)
'Albina Plena'	White	A new variety introduced in 1998	
'Ballet Skirt'	Pale pink looking	Slightly larger flowers, very full	
'Blue Bird'	Lavender-blue	Very large flowers	
macropetala 'Chili' formerly 'Harry Smith'	Pale greyish-blue, open, bell-shaped	Shorter sepals	
'Floriala'	Powder-blue often initially tinged green	A hybrid of C. macropetala x C. ochotensis	
'Jan Lindmark'	Rosy-mauve with deeper rose streaks	A seedling of 'Blue Bird'	
macropetala 'Lagoon'	Deep blue		
macropetala 'Maidwell Hall'	Navy-blue, often edged white	Semi-double bells	

C. macropetala forms attractive, shaggy seed heads

Variety	Colour	Features	Height (approx.)
macropetala 'Markham's Pink'	Clear bright pink	Full double appearance	2–2.5m (6½–8ft) (applies to all varieties)
'Pearl Rose'	Palest pink with deeper pink at base of sepals	A beautiful variety	
macropetala 'Purple Spider'	Deep purple	Flowers in profusion	
'Rosy O'Grady'	Rose-pink veined in mauve	Long, pointed sepals	
macropetala 'Snowbird'	White	Full double, slightly curled sepals	
'Vicky'	Pink with silvery margins	Finely cut foliage	
macropetala 'Westleton'	Mid-blue, cream inside	Flowers larger than type	
'White Lady'	Pure white	Flowers in profusion	
'White Moth'	White	Flowers larger than type	
'White Swan'	Creamy-white	Twisted sepals	

C. macropetala 'Markham's Pink', a dainty clematis for spring

C. MONTANA

Flowering season: May–June (unless stated otherwise)

Flowers: Open, single, 5–10cm (2–4in), scented

Aspect: Any (unless stated otherwise). Vigorous, requires lots of space. Suitable for growing into trees, over buildings, large walls and fences

Cultivation: Hardy; follow recommended planting and feeding programme

Pruning: Category 1. None required, because flowers are formed on previous year's growth. If necessary, prune immediately after flowering to contain growth

Background: *C. montana* species was originally introduced in the early part of the nineteenth century from the Himalayas, followed by other varieties from India and China. Many beautiful cultivars and hybrids have since been raised

The sweetly scented *C. montana* 'Elizabeth'

The bronze
foliage of
C. montana
'Broughton Star'
complements the
deep pink
double flowers

Variety	Colour	Features	Height (approx.)
C. montana	White	Profusion of flowers	6–10m (19½–33ft)
'Alba'	Creamy white	Light green foliage	6–10m (19½–33ft)
'Alexander'	White, larger flowers	Provide a sunny site to help establish this slow starter. Very sweet scent	6–10m (19½–33ft)
'Broughton Star'	Deep pink with cream stamens	Double flowers. Purple-bronze foliage	5–6.5m (16½–21ft)
C. chrysocoma	White with pink edges	Well-formed leaves with golden hairs. Shrubby	2–2.5m (6½–8ft)
'Elizabeth'	Pink	Vanilla scent; sunny site for perfume	6–10m (19½–33ft)
'Fragrant Spring'	Pink	Very sweetly scented. Attractive bronze foliage	6–10m (19½–33ft)
'Freda'	Cherry-pink with cream stamens	Bronze foliage	4–5m (13–16½ft)
'Gothenburg'	Pink with cream stamens	Deep green foliage with silver stripe. Flowers on long stalks	6–10m (19½–33ft)
'Grandiflora'	White with bright yellow anthers	Large flowers in profusion. Deep grey-green foliage	6–10m (19½–33ft)
'Jacqui'	White	Single, semi- and fully double. Heavily scented	5–6m (16½–19½ft)
'Lilacina'	Pink, flushed lilac-blue	A hybrid of 'Grandiflora' x 'Rubens'	6–10m (19½–33ft)
'Margaret Jones'	Pure white	Double flowers	10m (33ft)

C. montana 'Grandiflora' with *Vinca*, an evergreen, trailing perennial, more commonly known as periwinkle

Variety	Colour	Features	Height (approx.)
'Marjorie'	Salmon-pink with darker markings	Semi-double. Sunny site to develop full colour	10m (33ft)
'Mayleen'	Pink	Wavy-edged sepals; bronze foliage. Sweetly scented	6–10m (19½–33ft)
'New Dawn'	Bright pink	Broad sepals	6–10m (19½–33ft)
'Odorata'	Palest pink	Very sweet scent	6–10m (19½–33ft)
'Peveril'	Pure white with yellow stamens	Flowers later than type – July; flowers on long stalks	5–6m (16½–19½ft)
'Picton's Variety'	Deep rose-pink	Attractive bronze foliage	5m (16½ft)
'Pink Perfection'	Deep pink	Deep red stems; dark foliage	6–10m (19½–33ft)
'Rubens'	Deep pink with gold stamens	One of the most widely grown of the *montana* group	6–10m (19½–33ft)
'Spoonerii'	White with gold stamens	Hairy foliage	6–10m (19½–33ft)
'Superba'	Pink	Flowers larger than type	6–10m (19½–33ft)
'Tetrarose'	Deep lilac-pink	Attractive bronze foliage. Delicate spicy scent	6m (19½ft)
'Vera'	Pink	Large blooms. Very sweetly scented	6m (19½ft)
'Warwickshire Rose'	Deep pink	Unusual dark red foliage	6m (19½ft)
'Wilsonii'	White with cream-yellow sepals	An unusual variety with twisted sepals. Flowers later: June–July	6–10m (19½–33ft)

EARLY TO MID-SEASON, LARGE-FLOWERED CULTIVARS

Flowering season: Early varieties: May–June and September; Mid-season varieties: June–September

Flowers: Mostly saucer shaped, 10–20cm (4–8in), single, semi-double and fully double

Aspect: Any (unless stated). Pale colours can fade in full sun. Late frosts can damage early top growth

Cultivation: Follow recommended planting and feeding instructions outlined in Chapter 2. Carefully train the young shoots to grow horizontally as well as vertically or flowers will be all above eye level

Pruning: Early varieties: Category 2 – light prune only, because flowers are formed on previous year's growth; mid-season varieties: optional light, hard or partial pruning, depending on the situation. *Note:* Mid-season varieties are marked with abbreviation 'ms'. Follow recommended pruning instructions in Chapter 2

Background: Most species were discovered by the end of the nineteenth century. Cross-breeding has resulted in many beautiful new varieties. Their large blooms can bring a spectacular early show to the garden with the added bonus of a second flush in the early autumn. Mid-season varieties bloom continuously from June

'Joan Picton' flowers in early summer and autumn

Variety	Colour	Features	Height (approx.)
'Akaishi'	Deep purple with carmine stripes	Very large flowers; Japanese origin	2.5–3m (8–10ft)
'Alabast'	Cream with yellow anthers	Plant in semi-shade to protect colouring. Second flush in August	2.5–3m (8–10ft)
'Alice Fisk'	Pale blue with brown stamens	Large flowers	2–2.5m (6½–8ft)
'Allanah' (ms)	Ruby-red with brown stamens	Very large flowers June–September	3–4m (10–13ft)
'Andromeda'	White with vivid pink stripes	Early flowers are semi-double. Single flowers in September	2.5–3m (8–10ft)
'Anna'	Silvery-pink with pale pink stripes	Plant in shade to protect delicate colouring	2–2.5m (6½–8ft)
'Annabel' (ms)	Powder-blue with cream stamens	Flowers from June–September	2.5–3m (8–10ft)
'Anna Louise'	Purple with bold red stripes	Very large flowers. Seond flush can be as early as August	2–2.5m (6½–8ft)
'Arctic Queen'	White	Large, fully double flowers	2.5–3m (8–10ft)
'Asagasumi'	Pearly-white with pale lilac at centre of the sepals and cream stamens	Plant in semi-shade to protect delicate colouring	2.5–3m (8–10ft)
'Asao'	Deep pink with white bars	Another lovely variety from Japan	2–2.5m (6½–8ft)

The large flowers of C. 'Anna Louise' provide a bright display for many weeks

C. 'Asao', a popular Japanese ladies' name for a lovely Japanese-bred hybrid

C. 'Barbara Dibley' has large, petunia-red flowers that tend to fade in bright sunlight

C. 'Barbara Jackman' has lovely cream stamens offset by dramatic carmine stripes

Variety	Colour	Features	Height (approx.)
'Barbara Dibley'	Petunia-red with deeper stripes	Pointed sepals	2–2.5m (6½-8ft)
'Barbara Jackman'	Mauve-blue with carmine stripes and cream stamens	Named after the wife of Rowland Jackman, a famous breeder	2–2.5m (6½–8ft)
'Beauty of Richmond' (ms)	Pale mauve with deep blue bars	Flowers June–September	2.5–3m (8–10ft)
'Beauty of Worcester'	Deep blue with white centre	Large, fully double flowers, single in September	2–2.5m (6½–8ft)
'Bees Jubilee'	Pale mauve-pink with deeper pink stripes	Good second flowering in September	2–2.5m (6½–8ft)
'Belle Nantaise' (ms)	Pale lavender-blue with prominent cream stamens	Very large flowers June–September	3–4m (10–13ft)
'Belle of Woking'	Silver-lilac with yellow stamens	Heavy heads best supported by growing through shrubs	2–2.5m (6½–8ft)
'Bessie Watkinson'	Mid-blue with mauve shading on sepals	Large flowers	2.5–3m (8–10ft)

Variety	Colour	Features	Height (approx.)
'Betty Risdon'	Plum, edged in creamy-pink	Beautifully formed flower	2.5–3m (8–10ft)
'Black Madonna'	Deep violet purple with red stamens	Very free-flowering	2.5–3m (8–10ft)
'Blue Gem'	Lavender-blue with deep blue veining	Overlapping sepals form a rounded flower	2.5–3m (8–10ft)
'Blue Ravine'	Mauve-blue with deeper veining, contrasting purple and white stamens	Very free-flowering	2–2.5m (6½–8ft)
'Bracebridge Star'	Pale mauve with carmine stripes	Large, well-spaced sepals	2.5–3m (8–10ft)
'Candy Stripe'	Lilac-pink with rose-pink stripes	Grows well in any aspect	2.5–3m (8–10ft)
'Capitaine Thuilleaux'	Cream with bright pink stripes. Crimson anthers	Best grown in semi-shade	2.5–3m (8–10ft)
'Carnaby'	Deep pink with pale edges	Compact and free-flowering, ideal for containers	2m (6½ft)
'Carnival Queen'	Pale pink with cerise stripes	Large, open flowers	2.5–3m (8–10ft)

C. 'Charissima' has very large flowers and can be grown in sun or semi-shade

C. 'Corona', an early-flowering hybrid that can be grown in any aspect

Variety	Colour	Features	Height (approx.)
'Caroline'	Soft pink	One of the new hybrids	2.5–3m (8–10ft)
'Chalcedony'	Ice-blue with gold stamens	Fully double flowers early and late season. A dramatic show	2.5–3m (8–10ft)
'Charissima'	Cerise-pink with deep pink stripes	Long, pointed sepals	2.5–3m (8–10ft)
'Colette Deville'	Deep pink-mauve	Well-spaced sepals	3–4m (10–13ft)
'Corona'	Crimson, edged in purple	A compact plant suitable for containers	2m (6½ft)
'Countess of Lovelace'	Lilac-blue	Double flowers early, single later	2.5–3m (8–10ft)
'Crimson King' (ms)	Crimson with white filaments and brown anthers	A long flowering season, June–September	2.5–3m (8–10ft)
'C. W. Dowman'	Very pale pink with reddish-pink stripes	Plant in semi-shade to protect delicate colouring	2.5–3m (8–10ft)
'Daniel Deronda'	Violet-blue with sepals fading to a very pale blue	Occasional semi-double early flowers, single later	2.5–3m (8–10ft)
'Dawn'	Pearly-pink with prominent purple anthers	Plant in shade to protect delicate colouring	2.5–3m (8–10ft)
'Debutante'	Shocking pink	Plant in shade to prevent fading	2–2.5m (6½–8ft)
'Denny's Double'	Pale lavender-blue	Fully double flowers	2–2.5m (6½–8ft)
'Directeur André Devillers'	Pale blue	Large flowers	2–2.5m (6½–8ft)
'Dr. Ruppel'	Rose-pink with paler margins and cerise stripes	Strong-growing variety	2.5–3m (8–10ft)
'Dorothy Tolver'	Mauve-pink with yellow anthers	Occasionally semi-double	3–4m (10–13ft)
'Dorothy Walton'	Mauve with pink-mauve mottling	Long, pointed sepals	3–4m (10–13ft)

C. 'Duchess of Edinburgh', an early-flowering double with unusual leaves

C. 'Ernest Markham' will flower for a very long period if only half of the stems are pruned

Variety	Colour	Features	Height (approx.)
'Duchess of Edinburgh'	White with prominent golden stamens	Fully double flowers with unusual mottled white leaves below flower	2–2.5m (6½–8ft)
'Duchess of Sutherland' (ms)	Carmine with cream stamens	Flowers June–September	2.5–3m (8–10ft)
'Edith' (ms)	Creamy-white with maroon anthers	Very free-flowering, June–September. A good choice for containers	2–2.5m (6½–8ft)
'Edomurasaki'	Deep purple with rich red stamens	Name means old Edo (Tokyo) purple	2.5–3m (8–10ft)
'Edouard Desfossé'	Pale blue with blue-mauve stripes, purple anthers	Compact and free-flowering. Ideal for containers	2m (6½ft)
'Elsa Späth' (ms)	Violet-blue with red stamens	Flowers June–September	2–2.5m (6½–8ft)
'Empress of India' (ms)	Mauve-red with bright red stripes	Large flowers June–September	2.5–3m (8–10ft)
'Ernest Markham' (ms)	Rich red with golden stamens	Prune half of the stems hard to have flowers June–October	3–4m (10–13ft)
'Etoile de Malicorne'	Deep mauve with subtle paler mauve stripes	Grows well in any aspect	2.5–3m (8–10ft)

Variety	Colour	Features	Height (approx.)
'Etoile de Paris'	Violet-blue with deeper stripes	Large flowers with short, pointed sepals create distinctive appearance	2–2.5m (6½–8ft)
'Fair Rosamond' (ms)	Bluish white tinged with pale pink bars	Lightly scented flowers June–September. Plant in semi-shade to prevent fading	2–2.5m (6½–8ft)
'Fairy Queen' (ms)	Pale pink with deeper pink stripes	Flowers June–September. Plant in semi-shade to prevent fading	3–4m (10–13ft)
'Fireworks'	Purple with reddish-mauve stripes	Unusual kinked sepals	2.5–3m (8–10ft)
'Fujimusume'	Bright sky-blue	Compact and free-flowering over a long period	2–2.5m (6½–8ft)
'Gabrielle'	Lilac-blue with pale base to sepals	Free-flowering over a long period	2.5–3m (8–10ft)
'General Sikorski' (ms)	Mauve-blue with gold stamens	Large flowers have satin effect and do not fade; June–September	2.5–3m (8–10ft)
'Gillian Blades'	White, initially tinged mauve, with golden-yellow stamens	Sepals have attractive wavy edges	2–2.5m (6½–8ft)

C. 'General Sikorski', a very free-flowering, mid-season hybrid

The pure white flowers of C. 'Gillian Blades' measure 17–22cm (6½–8½in) across

Variety	Colour	Features	Height (approx.)
'Gladys Picard' (ms)	White, tinged blue	Large flowers June–September	2.5–3m (8–10ft)
'Glynderek'	Deep blue	Double flowers, but single later	2.5–3m (8–10ft)
'Guernsey Cream'	Cream with green stripes on first opening	Plant in semi-shade to protect delicate colour	2.5–3m (8–10ft)
'Haku Ookan'	Violet-purple with prominent creamy-white stamens	Compact	2–2.5m (6½–8ft)
'Hanaguruma'	Pink-red with yellow stamens	Sepals overlap to form a rounded flower	2–2.5m (6½–8ft)
'Helen Cropper'	Pale pink with irregular deep pink markings	Large flowers	2–2.5m (6½–8ft)
'Henryi' (ms)	Creamy-white with brown anthers	Large flowers June–September	3–3.5m (10–11½ft)
'Herbert Johnson' (ms)	Reddish-purple with maroon anthers	Flowers June–September	2.5–3m (8–10ft)
'H. F. Young'	Wedgwood-blue with cream stamens	Good choice for containers	2–2.5m (6½–8ft)
'Hikarugenji'	Bright lavender-blue with golden stamens	Fully double	2–2.5m (6½–8ft)
'Horn of Plenty'	Rosy-mauve with deep red centre	Large, attractive flowers	2.5–3m (8–10ft)
'Hybrida Sieboldii' (ms)	Clear lavender-blue with red stamens	Large flowers June–September	3–4m (10–13ft)
'Imperial'	Pale purple-pink fading to white at edges. Deep pink anthers	Large flowers; free-flowering	2.5–3m (8–10ft)
'Ishobel'	White, initially tinged blue	Attractive wavy-edged sepals	2.5–3m (8–10ft)

C. 'Henryi' has very large blooms which it produces from June to September

The large flowers of C. 'Horn of Plenty' look spectacular in sun or semi-shade

Variety	Colour	Features	Height (approx.)
'Ivan Olsen'	Ice-blue edged slightly deeper blue; purple anthers	Large flowers	2.5–3m (8–10ft)
'James Mason'	White with deep red anthers	Large flowers with attractive wavy edges	2–2.5m (6½–8ft)
'Jim Hollis'	Silvery blue	Double flowers early, single later	2.5–3m (8–10ft)
'Joan Gray'	Pale pink with deeper pink stripes	Double flowers early, single later. Plant in semi-shade to protect delicate colour	2.5–3m (8–10ft)
'Joan Picton'	Very pale lilac, edged in deeper lilac	Large flowers	2.5–3m (8–10ft)
'John Paul II' (ms)	Cream with pale pink stripes and red stamens	Plant in semi-shade to protect delicate colour. Flowers June–September	2.5–3m (8–10ft)
'John Warren' (ms)	Pale silvery-pink with deeper pink stripes	Plant in semi-shade to protect delicate colour. Flowers June–September	2.5–3m (8–10ft)

Variety	Colour	Features	Height (approx.)
Josephine (Evijohill')	Cream with deeper cream stamens	This lovely, unusual early variety can be seen at the British Clematis Society Gardens	2.5–3m (8–10ft)
'Kakio' ('Pink Champagne')	Pink with white central bars	Good choice for containers	2.5–3m (8–10ft)
'Kardynal Wysznski'	Deep red with gold stamens	Flowers July–September	2.5–3m (8–10ft)
'Kasugayama'	Bright lavender-blue with deep red anthers	Good choice for containers	2–2.5m (6½–8ft)
'Kathleen Dunford'	Rosy-purple with golden stamens	Large semi-double flowers early, single later	2.5–3m (8–10ft)
'Kathleen Wheeler' (ms)	Powdery mauve with cream stamens	Very large flowers June–September	2.5–3m (8–10ft)
'Keith Richardson'	Crimson flowers with red stripes	Hybrid of 'Barbara Dibley' x 'Lincoln Star'	2.5–3m (8–10ft)
'Ken Donson'	Deep blue with gold stamens	Hybrid of 'Barbara Jackman' x 'Daniel Deronda'	2.5–3m (8–10ft)
'King Edward VII' (ms)	Mauve-pink with red anthers	Very large flowers June–September	2.5–3m (8–10ft)
'King George V' (ms)	Very pale pink with shocking pink stripes	A feature plant when well placed. Blooms June–September	2–2.5m (6½–8ft)
'Kiri Te Kanawa'	Deep blue	Fully double flowers early and later	2–2.5m (6½–8ft)
'Königskind'	Pale violet with deep purple anthers	Very free-flowering. Good choice for containers	2–2.5m (6½–8ft)
'Lady Caroline Nevill' (ms)	Pale lavender-blue with white bars and red stamens	Semi-double flowers early, single later. Flowers June–September	3–4m (10–13ft)
'Lady in Red'	Cerise flushed with orange	Introduced at Chelsea in 1994	2.5–3m (8–10ft)
'Lady Londesborough'	Pale silvery-mauve	Plant in sheltered position and and semi-shade to prevent fading	2–2.5m (6½–8ft)
'Lady Northcliffe' (ms)	Deep blue with cream stamens	Flowers June–September	2–2.5m (6½–8ft)
'Lasurstern'	Mid-blue with yellow stamens	Large flowers	3–4m (10–13ft)
'Lavender Lace'	Lavender-blue flushed with mauve	Large flowers	2–2.5m (6½–8ft)

C. Guernsey Cream, a rare beauty which can be seen at the British Clematis Society Gardens, Bourne Hall, Surrey

The attractive mid-blue flowers and yellow stamens of C. 'Lasurstern' has made it an understandably popular early-flowering hybrid

Variety	Colour	Features	Height (approx.)
'Lawsoniana'	Pale blue with rosy tint; beige anthers	Very large flowers	2.5–3m (8–10ft)
'Lemon Chiffon'	Creamy, almost yellow on first opening. Yellow stamens	Plant in semi-shade to protect colouring	2–2.5m (6½–8ft)
'Liberation'	Deep cerise-pink fading at edges to pale pink with cream stamens	Prominent stamens	2.5–3m (8–10ft)
lilacina floribunda	Deep lilac-purple with reddish-brown anthers	Unusual twisted sepals	2.5–3m (8–10ft)
'Lilac Time'	Wisteria-blue, flecked with darker blue	Semi-double flowers early, single later	2–2.5m (6½–8ft)
'Lincoln Star'	Raspberry-pink with red anthers		2.5–3m (8–10ft)
'Lord Nevill'	Bright royal blue	Prefers a southerly aspect	2.5–3m (8–10ft)
'Louise Rowe'	Pale lilac with cream stamens	Fully double, semi-double and single can often flower at the same time. Semi-shade location	2–2.5m (6½–8ft)
'Marmut'	White with red anthers	Very large flowers	3–4m (10–13ft)

C. lilacina floribunda has unusual twisted sepals giving it quite a quirky character

C. 'Marie Boisselot' is very vigorous and flowers prolifically over a long period

Variety	Colour	Features	Height (approx.)
'Marcel Moser'	Pale pink with deeper pink stripes	Plant in semi-shade to protect delicate colouring	2.5–3m (8–10ft)
'Margaret Wood'	White with reddish-brown anthers	Large flowers	2.5–3m (8–10ft)
'Marie Boisselot' (ms)	White with gold stamens	Large flowers from June–September; vigorous	3–4m (10–13ft)
'Marie Louise Jensen'	Violet-blue	Long, pointed sepals	2–2.5m (6½–8ft)
'Marwood x'	Rich purple with matching anthers	Cross between 'Lasursten' and 'Mrs. N. Thompson'.	2–2.5m (6½–8ft)
'Masquerade'	Blue-mauve with rosy bars	Compact and very free-flowering	2–2.5m (6½–8ft)
'Maureen' (ms)	Deep red-purple	Large flowers June–September, compact and free-flowering. Good for containers	2–2.5m (6½–8ft)
'Miriam Markham'	Greyish-lilac	Double flowers	2–2.5m (6½–8ft)
'Miss Bateman'	White with reddish-brown stamens	Flowers May–June and occasionally later	2–2.5m (6½–8ft)
'Miss Crawshay'	Pale mauve-pink	Semi-double early, single later	2.5–3m (8–10ft)
'Monte Cassino'	Glowing red with cream stamens	Large flowers	2.5–3m (8–10ft)

Variety	Colour	Features	Height (approx.)
'Moonlight'	Cream with a hint of greenish-yellow	Plant in semi-shade for best colouring	2.5–3m (8–10ft)
'Mrs. Bush' (ms)	Pale mauve with beige anthers	Very large flowers June–September	2.5–3m (8–10ft)
✓ 'Mrs. Cholmondley' (ms)	Pale lavender-blue with mauve veining	Free-flowering May–September	3–4m (10–13ft)
'Mrs. George Jackman'	Creamy-white with pale brown anthers and white filaments	Semi-double flowers early, single later	2.5–3m (8–10ft)
'Mrs. Hope' (ms)	Bright blue with red stamens	Large flowers from June–September	3–4m (10–13ft)
'Mrs. James Mason'	Rich violet-blue with reddish-mauve stripes	Very large semi-double flowers early, single later	2–2.5m (6½–8ft)
'Mrs. N. Thompson'	Deep purple with very bright red stripe	Flowers May-June and August	2–2.5m (6½–8ft)

C. 'Masquerade' is compact and free-flowering. It is an ideal choice for a small garden

C. 'Marwood x' can be seen at Marwood Hill Gardens, north Devon

The cream stamens and pale blue sepals of C. 'Mrs. P. B. Truax' make it a delightful plant to have in the garden in late spring

C. 'Nelly Moser' has been popular for more than 100 years. She should be planted in semi-shade to prevent her vibrant colours from fading

Variety	Colour	Features	Height (approx.)
'Mrs. P. B. Truax'	Pale blue with cream stamens	Cup-shaped flowers	2.5–3m (8–10ft)
'Mrs. Spencer Castle'	Mauve-pink with gold stamens	Large semi-double flowers early, single later	2–2.5m (6½–8ft)
'Multi Blue'	Deep blue with silver reverse	Large double, semi-double and single flowers, early and late	2–2.5m (6½–8ft)
'Myojo'	Bluish-red with deep red stripes and cream stamens	Velvety texture	2–2.5m (6½–8ft)
'Natacha'	Pale lilac-pink; deep mauve stripes; reddish-purple anthers	Large flowers	2–2.5m (6½–8ft)
'Nelly Moser'	Pale mauve-pink with striking pink stripes	Plant in north-facing site or in shade to protect flowers from fading	3–4m (9–13ft)
'Olimpiada-80' (ms)	Bright mauve-red with yellow anthers	Large flowers June–September	2.5–3m (8–10ft)

Variety	Colour	Features	Height (approx.)
'Parasol' (ms)	Pale pink with irregular deep pink stripes	Large flowers June–September	2–2.5m (6½–8ft)
patens (Chinese form)	Very pale blue with prominent red anthers	One of the large-flowered species used in early hybridizing	2–2.5m (6½–8ft)
patens (Japanese form)	Deeper blue with red anthers	Grows well in sun or semi-shade	2–2.5m (6½–8ft)
'Patricia Ann Fretwell'	Pink with deeper pink edges	A new and stunning addition to the early double varieties	2–2.5m (6½–8ft)
'Peveril Pearl'	Silvery-lilac with deeper bars	Plant in semi-shade to protect flowers from fading	2–2.5m (6½–8ft)
'Prince Philip'	Rosy-mauve with reddish-pink bars	The tapering sepals have wavy edges	2.5–3m (8–10ft)
'Princess of Wales' (ms)	Pale mauve	Large satin-like flowers June–September	2.5–3m (8–10ft)
'Prins Hendrik' (ms)	Bright mauve-blue with purple anthers	Large flowers with wavy edges June–August	2–2.5m (6½–8ft)
'Proteus'	Lilac-rose pink	Fully double flowers early, single later	2.5–3m (8–10ft)
'Queen Alexandra'	Pale violet-blue	Very free-flowering. Good choice for containers	2–2.5m (6½–8ft)
'Ramona'	Lavender-blue	Flowers have satiny effect	2–2.5m (6½–8ft)
'Richard Pennell'	Reddish-purple with gold anthers	Large flowers	2.5–3m (8–10ft)
'Royalty'	Rosy-mauve with paler mauve-blue bars	Double flowers early, single later. Good choice for containers	2–2.5m (6½–8ft)
'Royal Velvet'	Deep purple-blue with red anthers	Velvety effect. Good choice for containers	2–2.5m (6½–8ft)
'Ruby Glow' (ms)	Mauve-red with ruby-red bars. Deep red anthers	Large flowers June–September	2.5–3m (8–10ft)
'Samantha Denny'	Pale blue	Large, fully double flowers early, single later	2–2.5m (6½–8ft)
'Satsukibare'	Mauve-blue with red shading at the tips	A beautiful, free-flowering Japanese variety	2.5–3m (8–10ft)

'Patricia Ann Fretwell' is a new double, early hybrid providing a spectacular show

The delicately coloured C. 'Special Occasion' blooms between June and August

Variety	Colour	Features	Height (approx.)
'Saturn'	Lavender-blue with soft mauve bars	Very large flowers	2.5–3m (8–10ft)
'Scartho Gem' (ms)	Bright pink with paler edges and deep anthers	Flowers June–September. A good choice for containers	2–2.5m (6½–8ft)
'Sealand Gem' (ms)	Pale pearly grey-mauve with reddish-mauve stripes	Occasional semi-double on old wood; June–September	2.5–3m (8–10ft)
'Serenata' (ms)	Deep purple with creamy-yellow stamens	Large flowers June–September	2.5–3m (8–10ft)
'Sho-un' (ms)	Lavender-blue with deeper blue veins and white stamens	Very large flowers June–September	2–2.5m (6½–8ft)
'Signe'	Pale violet with soft rosy bars	Large flowers	2.5–3m (8–10ft)
'Silver Moon' (ms)	Silver-grey with yellow stamens	Large flowers June–September	2.5–3m (8–10ft)

Variety	Colour	Features	Height (approx.)
'Sir Garnet Wolseley'	Mauve-purple with reddish-purple anthers	Compact and free-flowering. A good choice for containers	2–2.5m (6½–8ft)
'Snow Queen'	White, initially tinged mauve; red stamens	Large, wavy-edged flowers	2.5–3m (8–10ft)
'Souvenir de J. L. Delbard'	Bright blue with purple stripes	Grows well in sun or semi-shade	2.5–3m (8–10ft)
'Special Occasion' (ms)	Very pale pink with slightly deeper flush; reddish-brown anthers	Large flowers June–August	2–2.5m (6½–8ft)
'Sugar Candy' (ms)	Pink-mauve with deeper pink stripes, yellow anthers	Flowers June–September	2.5–3m (8–10ft)
'Sunset' (ms)	Glowing mauve-red with bright golden-yellow stamens	Flowers June–September	2.5–3m (8–10ft)
'Sylvia Denny'	White with creamy-yellow stamens	Double flowers early, single later. Strongly scented	2.5–3m (8–10ft)
'Sympathia' (ms)	Rosy-mauve with reddish-brown stamens	Large flowers June–September	2–2.5m (6½–8ft)
'Tateshina'	Violet-blue with rosy-mauve bars and yellow stamens	Compact and free-flowering. A good choice for containers	2–2.5m (6½–8ft)
'Tazuki'	Pure white with bright yellow stamens	Striking Japanese variety	2–2.5m (6½–8ft)
'Teshio'	Lavender-blue	Double flowers develop from spider-like buds. A lovely and unusual variety. Compact and free-flowering. Good choice for containers	2–2.5m (6½–8ft)
'The Bride' (ms)	White with cream stamens	Large flowers June–September	2–2.5m (6½–8ft)

C. 'The President' was introduced in 1876 and is now one of the most popular hybrids

C. 'William Kennet' has a lovely two-tone effect as the sepals fade

Variety	Colour	Features	Height (approx.)
'The President' (ms)	Deep purple with red anthers	Large flowers June–September	2.5–3m (8–10ft)
'The Vagabond'	Deep burgundy with purple stripes; creamy-yellow stamens	Very compact. Good choice for containers	1.5–2m (5–6½ft)
'Titania' (ms)	White with reddish-pink stripes. Deep maroon anthers with white filaments	Exceptionally large flowers June–September	2.5–3m (8–10ft)
'Trianon'	Bright red with deeper bars and deep red anthers	Named after the royal villas in the gardens of Louis XIIII in Versailles	2–2.5m (6½–8ft)
'Twilight'	Mauve-pink fading at the edges; yellow stamens	Very free-flowering	2–2.5m (6½–8ft)
'Veronica's Choice'	Very pale lavender streaked with a very soft rosy-lilac	Double flowers in May and June. Plant in semi-shade	2.5–3m (8–10ft)

Variety	Colour	Features	Height (approx.)
'Vino'	Bright red with cream stamens	Flowers almost continuously May–September	2.5–3m (8–10ft)
'Violet Charm' (ms)	Intense violet-blue with red stamens	Flowers June–September	2–2.5m (6½–8ft)
'Violet Elizabeth'	Mauve-pink	Double flowers early, single later	2–2.5m (6½–8ft)
'Vyvyan Pennell'	Mauve-blue flushed with red	Large, fully double early flowers, single later	2.5–3m (8–10ft)
'Wada's Primrose'	Creamy-yellow	Large flowers scented like satsumas	2–2.5m (6½–8ft)
'Walter Pennell'	Greyish-mauve with carmine bars	Double flowers early, single later	2.5–3m (8–10ft)
'W. E. Gladstone' (ms)	Lilac-blue with purple stamens	Exceptionally large flowers June–September. Vigorous	3–4m (10–13ft)
'Wilhelmina Tull'	Deep purple with vivid red stripes	Large flowers. Strong growth	2.5–3m (8–10ft)
'Will Goodwin' (ms)	Pale lavender-blue with gold stamens	Wavy-edged flowers June–September	2.5–3m (8–10ft)
'William Kennet' (ms)	Deep mauve-blue with red stamens	The sun fades the flowers to give lovely two-tone effect. All summer	3–4m (10–13ft)
'W. S. Callick'	Bright red with red stamens	Hard prune half of the stems in February to give long flowering season	2.5–3m (8–10ft)
'Yvette Houry'	Pale blue	Very large double flowers early, single later	2.5–3m (8–10ft)

C. 'Vyvyan Pennell' adorning a pergola

A healthy, young, pot-grown C. 'Will Goodwin'

C. VITICELLA

Flowering season: July–September (unless stated otherwise)

Flowers: Open, bell shaped, 4–8cm (1½–3in) unless stated otherwise

Aspect: Any; particularly suited to growing through trees and shrubs, and a good choice for containers

Cultivation: Follow recommended planting, watering and feeding instructions outlined in Chapter 2

Pruning: Category 3. If blooms are required low down, or space is limited, hard prune, because flowers are formed on current year's growth. If grown through trees or tall shrubs, *viticella* types can be left unpruned and allowed to scramble to their full height

Background: *Clematis viticella* was introduced from Spain in the mid-sixteenth century. From the original species many cultivars and hybrids have been bred and continue to be raised by the many admirers of this valuable group

C. viticella 'Purpurea Plena Elegans'

Variety	Colour	Features	Height (approx.)
viticella	Mid-deep purple	Not widely grown even though it flowers profusely	4–5m (13–16½ft)
'Abundance'	Red-pink with deeper veins, creamy-green stamens	As the name suggests, a very free-flowering cultivar	2.5–3m (8–10ft)
'Alba Luxurians'	White with green-tipped sepals and deep purplish-black anthers	Attractive and unusual flower formation	2.5–3m (8–10ft)
'Betty Corning'	Creamy white, edged and veined in pale lilac	Very free-flowering and sweetly scented	2.5–3m (8–10ft)
'Black Prince'	Purple-black with green stamens	Flowers grow in more upright manner than type	2.5–3m (8–10ft)
'Blue Belle'	Deep purple with cream anthers	Larger flowers than type	3–4m (10–13ft)
'Cicciolina'	Deep pink-red with creamy-white stripes and cream anthers	A stunning variety	3–4m (10–13ft)
'Elvan'	Purple; cream stripes	Very free-flowering	3–4m (10–13ft)
'Entel'	Light violet with dark veins. Pale greenish-yellow anthers	A good companion for roses	2–3m (6½–10ft)
'Etoile Violette'	Deep purple; creamy-yellow stamens	Very free-flowering	3–4m (10–13ft)

C. viticella 'Alba Luxurians'

C. viticella 'Etoile Violette' gives masses of flowers

C. 'Kermesina'   C. *viticella* 'Mme Julia Correvon'

Variety	Colour	Features	Height (approx.)
'Foxtrot'	White edged in bluish-purple	A new cultivar ideal for growing through medium-sized shrubs	2.5–3m (8–10ft)
'Kermesina'	Deep wine-red with white spot at base of each sepal	Very free-flowering	3–4m (10–13ft)
'Little Nell'	White, edged in pale mauve; green stamens	Small, dainty flowers	3–4m (10–13ft)
'Madame Julia Correvon'	Rich vibrant red with gold stamens	Larger flowers than type; the sepals are twisted	2.5–3m (8–10ft)
'Margot Koster'	Mauve-pink	Open appearance with twisted sepals	2.5–3m (8–10ft)
'Mary Rose' (*viticella* 'Flore Pleno')	Deep greyish-purple	This cultivar is believed to be very old; known as *C. peregrina purpurea flore plena* in 1623 and the 'double purple virgins bower' when described in 1629. Re-introduced and re-named in recent years as 'Mary Rose'	2.5–3m (8–10ft)
'Minuet'	Cream, edged in rosy-mauve; green stamens	Grows well in any aspect	2.5–3m (8–10ft)
'Mrs. Lundell'	Bluish-lilac	Nodding flowers with slightly recurving sepals	2.5–3m (8–10ft)

Variety	Colour	Features	Height (approx.)
'Polish Spirit'	Rich purple-red with deep red anthers	Easy to grow; masses of blooms	3–4m (10–13ft)
'Purpurea Plena Elegans'	Dusky purple	Double flowers in profusion. Similar to 'Flora Pleno' ('Mary Rose')	3–4 m (10–13ft)
'Royal Velours'	Deep reddish-purple with matching anthers	Grows well in any aspect	3–4m (10–13ft)
'Rubra'	Deep crimson with brown stamens	Flowers in profusion	2.5–3m (8–10ft)
'Soldertalje'	Reddish-pink with green anthers	Nodding flowers	3–4m (10–13ft)
'Tango'	Cream, edged and veined in red	Similar to 'Minuet' but brighter	2.5–3m (8–10ft)
'Tentel'	Dark rosy-pink with greenish-yellow stamens	Frilled edges. Flowers in profusion	2–3m (6½–10ft)
'Venosa Violacea'	White, edged and veined in purple with very deep purple anthers	Larger flowers than type	2.5–3m (8–10ft)

C. viticella 'Margot Koster'

The flowers of *viticella* 'Minuet' are long-stemmed

LATE, LARGE-FLOWERED CULTIVARS

Flowering season: July–September; mid-season varieties: June–September

Flowers: Mostly saucer-shaped, 10–14cm (4–5½in) unless stated otherwise

Aspect: Any (unless stated otherwise)

Cultivation: Follow recommended planting, watering, and feeding instructions outlined in Chapter 2

Pruning: Category 3. Hard prune, because flowers are formed on current year's growth. Mid-season varieties: optional, hard prune or partial prune according to requirements. The mid-season hybrids shown in this category generally need a hard prune periodically to prevent them becoming leggy. Mid-season varieties are marked 'ms'

Background: Clematis within this group, like those of the early, large-flowered hybrids, are the result of breeding by clematis enthusiasts and specialists from many parts of the world. Most have been introduced during the past century. Unlike the early-flowering hybrids, however, choice is somewhat restricted

C. florida 'Alba Plena'

C. 'Comtesse de Bouchard', one of the most beautiful of the late-flowering hybrids

C. 'Gypsy Queen' produces deep purple flowers with a delightful velvet sheen

Variety	Colour	Features	Height (approx.)
'Ascotiensis' (ms)	Bright lavender-blue	Usually in flower during Ascot week. June–September	3–4m (10–13ft)
'Bella'	White, initially with cream stripes	Compact and free-flowering. Good choice for containers	2–2.5m (6½–8ft)
'Black Prince'	Deepest shade of purple, almost black, fading to reddish-purple	Interesting variety for lovers of very dark flowers	3–4m (10–13ft)
'Blue Angel' (Blekitny Aniol)	Sky-blue, with slightly darker edges	Sepals deeply furrowed with wavy edges	3–4m (10–13ft)
'Cardinal Wyszynski' (ms)	Crimson	Vigorous; flowers in profusion June–September	2.5–3m (8–10ft)
'Comtesse de Bouchard'	Mauve-pink	Flowers in profusion	3–4m (10–13ft)
'Dorothy Walton'	Mauve with pink-mauve mottling	Long, pointed sepals	3–4m (10–13ft)
florida 'Alba Plena' (ms)	Greenish-white	Fully double flowers; likes sunny position away from winds. A good choice for containers. Flowers June–September	2–2.5m (6½–8ft)
florida 'Sieboldii' (ms)	White with deep purple centres	Exotic, tender variety; ideal for container on patio or conservatory. Flowers June–September	2–2.5m (6½–8ft)

Variety	Colour	Features	Height (approx.)
'Gipsy Queen'	Deep purple with red anthers	Flowers in abundance; they have a velvet sheen	3–4m (10–13ft)
'Guiding Star'	Violet-blue	Nicely shaped flowers	2.5–3m (8–10ft)
'Hagley Hybrid'	Pale mauve-pink with reddish-brown anthers	Plant in shade to protect colouring	2m (6½ft)
'Huldine'	Pearly-white with pale pink on reverse	Thrives in full sun	3–4m (10–13ft)
'Jackmanii'	Deep purple with green stamens	Very free-flowering	3–4m (10–13ft)
'Jenny Caddick'	Reddish-mauve with cream stamens	A recent introduction	2.5–3m (8–10ft)
'John Huxtable'	White with creamy-yellow stamens	Very free-flowering	2.5–3m (8–10ft)
'Lady Betty Balfour'	Deep blue with creamy-yellow stamens	Plant in full sun for a long season; August–October	3m+ (10ft+)
'Lucey' (ms)	Mauve-pink with gold stamens	Flowers in profusion June–September	2–2½ft (6½–8ft)
'Madame Baron Veillard'	Lilac-pink with greenish-white stamens	Plant in full sun for a long season; August–October	3m+ (10ft+)

C. 'Hagley Hybrid' is a lovely translucent pink-mauve but will fade if planted in full sunlight

C. 'Jackmanii' is very free-flowering, raised by famous breeders George Jackman & Son in 1958

The edges of the sepals curl back on C. 'Madame Grangé' to reveal a lighter underside

C. 'Niobe' appears to be almost black when it opens, but lightens slightly as it matures

Variety	Colour	Features	Height (approx.)
'Madame Edouard André'	Deep wine-red with cream stamens	Prefers a southerly aspect	3–4m (10–13ft)
'Madame Grangé'	Deep rosy-purple with reddish-purple anthers	Edges of the sepals curl inwards	2.5–3m (8–10ft)
'Margaret Hunt'	Mauve-pink with reddish-brown anthers	Vigorous and free-flowering	3–4m (10–13ft)
'Miikla'	White with slight pink tinge and pinkish-green stripes	Flowers July-September. Name means riddle	3–4m (10–13ft)
'Monte Cassino'	Glowing red with cream stamens	May fade in strong sunlight, good light required, not a north wall	2.5–3m (8–10ft)
'Nikolaj Rubtzov'	Mauve-red with paler stripes and yellow anthers	Free-flowering	2.5–3m (8–10ft)
'Niobe'	Very deep red, almost black on opening; yellow stamens	A good variety for lovers of very dark flowers; June–September	2.5–3m (8–10ft)
'Perle d'Azur'	Light blue with pale greenish-yellow stamens	Very vigorous and free-flowering	3–4m (10–13ft)

'Perle d'Azur', a mass of delicate flowers for summer

Variety	Colour	Features	Height (approx.)
'Perrins Pride'	Purple with bronze anthers	Leave some stems unpruned as this variety produces larger flowers from old wood	2.5–3m (8–10ft)
'Pink Fantasy'	Pale pink with deeper pink stripes and brown anthers	Wavy-edged sepals	2–2.5ft (6½–8ft)
'Pohjanael'	Mid-blue with deeper bars	Spike effect at the end of the sepals	2.5–3m (8–10ft)
'Prince Charles'	Mauve-blue	Semi-nodding flowers on a free-flowering, compact plant. Good choice for containers	2–2.5ft (6½–8ft)
'Rouge Cardinal' (ms)	Velvet-red with beige anthers	Flowers in profusion June–September	2–2.5ft (6½–8ft)
'Sputnik' (ms)	Various shades of denim-blue	Very free-flowering June–October	3–4m (10–13ft)
'Star of India' (ms)	Deep purple with vivid red stripes	Flowers in profusion June–September	3–4m (10–13ft)
'Victoria' (ms)	Lilac-pink with buff stamens	Flowers June–October	3–4m (10–13ft)

Variety	Colour	Features	Height (approx.)
'Ville de Lyon' (ms)	Bright red, fading in the sun to silvery pink edged in red; gold stamens	Flowers June–September	3–4m (10–13ft)
'Viola'	Bluish-violet with greenish-yellow stamens	Medium-sized flowers	2.5–3m (8–10ft)
'Vivienne Lawson'	Violet-purple with gold anthers	Pointed sepals	2.5–3m (8–10ft)
'Voluceau' (ms)	Petunia-red with yellow anthers	Very free-flowering June–September	2.5–3m (8–10ft)
'Vostok'	Purple-mauve with subtle red bars	Velvet sheen with textured appearance	2.5–3m (8–10ft)
'Warsaw Nike'	Very deep purple with cream stamens	Another very dark variety	2.5–3m (8–10ft)
'Westerplatte' (ms)	Dark velvet-red with red stamens and yellow anthers	Flowers May–September. Distinctive velvety sheen	1m (3¼ft)

Clematis 'Rouge Cardinal' flowers in profusion throughout the summer

'Ville de Lyon'. The deeper margins become more pronounced as the sepals fade

HERBACEOUS SPECIES AND CULTIVARS

Flowering season: Varies between June and October

Flowers: Various shapes and sizes as stated

Aspect: Suitable for planting in a mixed border. Mostly they will tolerate any aspect

Cultivation: Follow recommended planting, watering and feeding instructions outlined in Chapter 2

Pruning: Most herbaceous clematis fit into Category 3. Like other herbaceous plants they naturally die back in the winter and only need to be trimmed and neatened. Small rockery plants which bloom early in the season may not require pruning and this will be stated

Background: Herbaceous clematis are mostly resultant of breeding from the species *integrifolia*, *recta* and *heracleifolia*. *Clematis integrifolia* and *recta* were introduced from Europe in the latter part of the sixteenth century. *Clematis heracleifolia* was discovered in northern China just into the second half of the nineteenth century. In the following list, the herbaceous clematis have been roughly grouped together by type

Clematis integrifolia will grow into a bushy plant about 60cm (2ft) high

C. integrifolia 'Rosea' is one of the loveliest of the herbaceous clematis

Variety	Colour	Features	Height (approx.)
integrifolia	Indigo-blue	Sweetly scented nodding flowers with twisted, recurving sepals. June–September	0.5–1m (2–3¼ft)
'Alba'	Pure white	Flowers June–September	0.5–1m (2–3¼ft)
'Amy'	Silvery-white, sky-blue on the inside	Sweetly scented. June–September	0.5–1m (2–3¼ft)
'Floris V'	Burgundy	Sweetly scented. June–September	0.5–1m (2–3¼ft)
eriostemon 'Hendersonii'	Deep blue	Star-shaped flowers in profusion. July–September	1.5–2m (5–6½ft)
'Lauren'	Deep lilac, edged in paler lilac-pink	Sweetly scented. June–September	1.5–1m (2–3¼ft)
'Olgae'	Mid-blue	Sweetly scented flowers with twisted sepals. June–September	1.5–1m (2–3¼ft)
'Pangbourne Pink'	Deep cerise-pink	Nodding flowers June–September	1.5–1m (2–3¼ft)
'Pastel Blue'	Pale powder blue	June–September	0.5–1m (2–3¼ft)
'Pastel Pink'	Flesh-pink	Nodding flowers with twisted recurving sepals. June–September	1.5–1m (2–3¼ft)
'Rosea'	Bright pink	Sweetly scented. June–September	1.5–1m (2–3¼ft)
'Tapestry'	Deep pink	June–September	1.5–1m (2–3¼ft)
heracleifolia davidiana	Lavender-blue	Hyacinth-like, sweetly scented. July–September	1–1.5m (3¼–5ft)
'Aljonushka'	Rose-pink	Nodding flowers, July–September	1.5–2m (5–6½ft)

This dainty scrambler, *x eriostemon* 'Hendersonii', is seen here growing through *Cytisus* (broom)

'Aljonushka', raised at the State Nikitsky Botanic Gardens, Crimea

Variety	Colour	Features	Height (approx.)
'Arabella'	Purple-blue with cream anthers	Good choice for containers or growing through small shrubs	1.5–2m (5–6½ft)
'Aromatica'	Deep violet-blue with yellow stamens	Plant in a sunny border. Sweetly scented. June–September	1.5–2m (5–6½ft)
'Campanile'	Pale blue with paler bars	Hyacinth-like flowers, July–September	1.5–2m (5–6½ft)
'Cote d'Azur'	Pale blue with white bars	Small flowers, July–September	1.5–2m (5–6½ft)
'Crepuscule'	Pale mauve	Small tubular flowers scented. July–September	1–1.5m (3¼–5ft)
brachyura	White with cream stamens	Small, scented flowers in profusion. A rare species from Korea. June–August	1.5–2m (5–6½ft)
'Durandii'	Indigo-blue with bright yellow stamens	A lovely clematis to grow through small shrubs and roses in the border. June–September	2–2.5m (6½–8ft)
'Edward Pritchard'	Cream, edged with caramel	Plant in full sunshine to draw out the magnificent scent. July–September	1.5–2m (5–6½ft)
hirsutissima var. scottii	Lavender-blue with cream stamens	Urn-shaped flowers. Sunny aspect. A rare species from the Rockies, USA. June–August	2–2.5m (6½–8ft)
ispahanica	White with deep red stamens	Small flowers with recurving sepals. From Iran	1.5–2m (5–6½ft)
'Joe' (formerly cartmanii 'Joe')	White	Small flowers in profusion in April. Good for rockery, in sun. Needs winter protection. Evergreen, finely cut foliage. Category 1: do not prune	0.5m (2ft)
jouiniana	Pale mauve	Flowers in large panicles, July–September. Good ground cover	2–2.5m (6½–8ft)
jouiniana 'Praecox'	Mauve-pink	An earlier-flowering form of 'Jouiniana', June–September	2–2.5m (6½–8ft)
mandshurica	White	Star-shaped flowers with an aniseed scent, in profusion, July–September	1.5–2m (5–6½ft)
'Mrs. Robert Brydon'	Grey-blue	A small, subtle flower. August–September	2–2.5m (6½–8ft)
'Petit Faucon'	Deep violet with yellow anthers	Semi-nodding flowers, July–September	1–1.5m (3¼–5ft)

C. 'Durandii' will scramble through the border or climb to 2.5m (8ft) if given support

C. jouiniana 'Praecox' is a lovely ground plant for the herbaceous border

Variety	Colour	Features	Height (approx.)
recta	Pure white	Sweetly scented flowers, in profusion, June–August. Needs support	1.5–2m (5–6½ft)
'Peveril'	Pure white	Scented flowers June–August. More compact than *recta*	1–1.5m (3¼–5ft)
'Purpurea'	White	Scented flowers, June–August. No doubt the deep purple new foliage inspired the name	1.5–2m (5–6½ft)
songarica	Pure white with yellow stamens	Flowers July–September, followed by attractive seed heads. Bamboo-like stems. Native of Siberia and Mongolia, introduced in late nineteenth century	1–1.5m (3¼–5ft)
stans	Blue	Tiny tubular flowers in profusion, August–October. Requires full sun to draw out the lily-of-the-valley scent. A rare species	1–1.5m (3¼–5ft)
'Rusalka'	Bright Wedgwood-blue	All of the beauty of *stans*, but with more delicate foliage and a dwarf habit	1m (3¼ft)
versicolor	Deep cherry-pink tips and white base	Small urn-shaped flowers July–September; striking seed heads. A rare species introduced from the USA, late nineteenth century	1.5–2m (5–6½ft)

C. ORIENTALIS

Flowering season: July–September, unless stated otherwise

Flowers: Nodding, bell-shaped or open, bell-shaped; followed by attractive seed heads, 2–4cm (¾–1½in)

Aspect: Sun or semi-shade

Cultivation: Follow recommended planting, watering and feeding instructions outlined in Chapter 2

Pruning: Category 3. Pruning is optional with this group. An effective method is to prune half the stems to the ground in April. The unpruned stems will have flowers at their full height whilst the new stems will flower low down

Background: Because of their nodding bell-shaped flowers in various shades of yellow, the following clematis have been grouped together. They are made up of *orientalis*, *tangutica* and *tibetana* species and their cultivars and hybrids. Due to cross breeding it is difficult to allocate them specifically. *Clematis tangutica* was introduced in the late nineteenth century having been found growing wild from north-west India to west China. *Clematis tibetana* was introduced a few years later and as the name suggests its homeland was Tibet. *Clematis orientalis* is a species from Afghanistan

'Bill Mackenzie' bears the largest flowers in the *orientalis* group

Clematis 'Bill Mackenzie' tumbles gracefully through *Escallonia* 'Iveyi'

Variety	Colour	Features	Height (approx.)
tangutica	Mid-yellow	Vigorous growth with abundant flowers, followed by large, fluffy seed heads	4–5m (13–16½ft)
'Aureolin'	Lemon-yellow	Flowers open wider than type	4–5m (13–16½ft)
'Bill Mackenzie'	Strong yellow	Larger flowers than type with recurving tips, followed by very large, fluffy seed heads	4–5m (13–16½ft)
'Burford Variety'	Deep yellow	Silvery seed heads	3–4m (10–13ft)
'Golden Harvest'	Yellow with purple stamens	Small, nodding flowers	3–4m (10–13ft)
'Gravetye Variety'	Bright yellow	Very fine foliage	4–5m (13–16½ft)
'Helios'	Bright yellow	Nodding flowers opening flat from May–September, very free-flowering; of low growth	1.5–2m (5–6½ft)
'Lambton Park'	Bright yellow	Large flowers followed by large seed heads	4–5m (13–16½ft)

▲ *Clematis* 'Orange Peel' and shrub rose 'Graham Thomas' create a warm, vibrant partnership

▶ The blue-green foliage of *C. x glauca akebioides* complements the dainty flower

Variety	Colour	Features	Height (approx.)
'Orange Peel'	Orange-yellow	Small, nodding flowers	4–5m (13–16½ft)
'Sheriffii'	Yellow	Large flowers and attractive foliage	4–5m (13–16½ft)
tibetana	Pale yellow	Small, nodding flowers	4–5m (13–16½ft)
'Vernayi'	Orange-yellow	Small, nodding flowers are somewhat sparse; attractive grey-blue, fine-cut foliage	4–5m (13–16½ft)
'Vernayi L & S 13342'	Yellow	Small, nodding flowers with very thick sepals	4–5m (13–16½ft)
'Laciniifolia'	Orange-yellow with maroon stamens	Small, nodding flowers	4–5m (13–16½ft)
var. *tenuifolia*	Bright yellow	Small, nodding flowers with reflexed sepals on long stalks. Flowers August–October	3–4m (10–13ft)
x glauca akebiodes	Orange-yellow with brown stamens	Flowers open almost fully with lovely blue-green foliage	3–4m (10–13ft)

C. TEXENSIS

Flowering season: July–October, unless stated otherwise

Flowers: Tulip shaped, 2–2.5cm (¾–1in) unless stated otherwise

Aspect: Sunny and preferably sheltered. They love to scramble and climb over other plants

Cultivation: Follow recommended planting, watering and feeding instructions outlined in Chapter 2

Pruning: Category 3. Hard prune, because flowers are formed on current year's growth. Like a perennial plant they will naturally die down in late autumn

Background: *Clematis texensis* was introduced from America in the latter part of the nineteenth century where it was found growing wild. The original species is still quite a rarity, but a number of hybrids have been raised to increase choice amongst these beautiful tulip-shaped, vibrantly coloured clematis

C. texensis species is a rare beauty

Variety	Colour	Features	Height (approx.)
texensis	Shades of red from deep cherry to vermilion and crimson	Small, urn-shaped flowers	2–2.5m (6½–8ft)
'Duchess of Albany'	Candy-pink with deeper bars	Flowers face upward; a good variety for scrambling through low shrubs or for a container	2–2.5m (6½–8ft)
'Etoile Rose'	Bright pink with silvery-pink margins	Good choice for growing over an archway	2.5–3m (8–10ft)
'Gravetye Beauty'	Rich deep red with matching stamens	These upward–facing flowers open wider than type	2.5–3m (8–10ft)
'Ladybird Johnson'	Purple-red with yellow stamens	Outward-facing flowers	2–2.5m (6½–8ft)

'Duchess of Albany' scrambles beautifully over evergreen shrub *Coprosma*

C. 'Etoile Rose' makes a dainty partner for campanula

Autumn sunshine captures the glowing red of 'Gravetye Beauty'

C. texensis 'Sir Trevor Lawrence'

Variety	Colour	Features	Height (approx.)
'Pagoda'	White with pink-mauve edges and veining	Flowers larger than type; they have four sepals which recurve to resemble a pagoda	2–2.5m (6½–8ft)
'Princess Diana' (formerly 'The Princess of Wales')	Deep vibrant pink with paler margins	Outward-facing, trumpet-shaped flowers, August–October	2–2.5m (6½–8ft)
'Sir Trevor Lawrence'	Red-purple with red stripes	Outward-facing flowers; sepals recurve slightly	2–2.5m (6½–8ft)
'Viorna'	Reddish-purple	Urn-shaped flowers. A rare *texensis* type	2–2.5m (6½–8ft)

LATE, SMALL-FLOWERED SPECIES AND CULTIVARS

Flowering season: Varies between June and October

Flowers: Mostly small, of various shapes, as stated

Aspect: Any, unless stated otherwise

Cultivation: Follow recommended planting, watering and feeding instructions outlined in Chapter 2

Pruning: Category 3. Hard prune, because flowers are formed on current year's growth

Background: There are a number of species within this group and the background, where known, is shown in the features column. There are a few rare and unusual varieties, which will appeal to the rare plant collector, but the mass of sweetly scented blooms for long summer months makes them a delightful addition to any garden

Almond-scented *flammula* will flower from July to October in a sunny border

Variety	Colour	Features	Height (approx.)
'Annemieke'	Yellow	Small, nodding flowers with twisted recurving sepals. July–September. Raised in Holland during recent years	3–4m (10–13ft)
apilifolia	Creamy-white with prominent cream stamens	Small, star-shaped flowers in profusion with bright-green foliage. Introduced from China in the late nineteenth century	4–5m (13–16½ft)
buchananiana	Creamy-yellow	Plant in sun to enhance small, scented flowers which grow in profusion, August–October. From the Himalayas	5–6m (16½–19½ft)
'Burford Bell'	Pale purple-blue	Small, nodding flowers July–October	2.5–3m (8–10ft)
campaniflora	White, tinged with blue	Dainty, nodding flowers July-September. Species from Portugal early nineteenth century	3–4m (10–13ft)

Variety	Colour	Features	Height (approx.)
chinensis	White	Small, star-shaped flowers July–September. Plant in sunny aspect to draw out sweet scent. From China mid-eighteenth century	3–4m (10–13ft)
connata	Yellow	Small, bell-shaped flowers with big, veined leaves. Sweet scent. Sunny aspect. From Tibet late nineteenth century	6m (19½ft)
crispa	Violet-blue, star-shaped, white inside	Small, bell-shaped flowers July–September, then spider-like seed heads. From America early eighteenth century	1.5–2m (5–6½ft)
crispa hybrid (Not yet named)	Dusky mauve-red; paler at the base of the sepals	Flowers larger than *crispa*, July–September	3–4m (10–13ft)
'Cylindrica'	Mauve-blue	Nodding flowers July–September. Hybrid of *integrifolia* and *crispa*	1–1.5m (3¼–5ft)
flammula	Pure white	Small, star-shaped flowers, July–October. Prune back by half. Plant in full sun. From southern Europe end sixteenth century	4–5m (13–16½ft)
fusca	Chocolate-brown	Small, urn-shaped flowers with short brown hairs June–September, then attractive seed heads. From N. E. Asia mid-nineteenth century	2–2.5m (6½–8ft)
fusca violacea	Purple	Small, urn-shaped flowers June–September followed by striking seed heads. Introduced from N. China late nineteenth century	2–2.5m (6½–8ft)
gouriana	Creamy-white	Small flowers August–October. Vigorous. From Nepal	4–5m (13–16½ft)
'Grace' (A hybrid of *serratifolia* x *ligusticifolia*)	Creamy-white with wine-red stamens	Flowers are held on long stalks. Originally raised in Canada early twentieth century	3–3.5m (10–11½ft)
grata	Creamy-white	Small flowers August–October. A rare species from China and Taiwan start twentieth century	8m (26ft)
hilariae	Bright yellow	Outward-facing flowers with twisted, recurving sepals July–September. Attractive seed heads. Rare, from Afghanistan	3–5m (10–16½ft)

Variety	Colour	Features	Height (approx.)
intricata (*akebiodes*)	Creamy-yellow, flushed maroon at base	Nodding flowers with twisted, recurving sepals, June–September. From China	3m (10ft)
kirilowii	White	Small, scented flowers July–September. Likes sunny position. Native of China	3–4m (10–13ft)
ladakhiana	Gold with bronze speckles	Small, nodding flowers with twisted, recurving sepals, August–October. From Kashmir	3–4m (10–13ft)
lasiandra	Reddish-purple	Small, nodding flowers with recurving sepals. August–September. Species found wild in Japan, China and Taiwan	2–2.5m (6½–8ft)
ligusticifolia	White	Small, star–shaped flowers, in profusion, July–September. North American species	6m (19½ft)
'Lisboa'	Pale mauve	Small flowers with recurving sepals. July–September. Raised at botanical gardens in Lisbon	2.5–3m (8–10ft)
'Paul Farges' (Summer Snow)	White	Small, sweetly scented flowers in profusion, July–September. Raised in Ukraine	5–6m (16½–19½ft)
peterae	Creamy-white	Small, scented flowers. Requires sunny position. From China	5m (16½ft)
pierotii	White	Small flowers, August–October. Sunny position to prolong flowering. Rare, from Japan	3–4m (10–13ft)
pitcheri	Deep pink-red on the outside, deep red inside	Urn-shaped nodding flowers, curled-back sepals. From west of America	2–2.5m (6½–8ft)
potanini	White with yellow anthers	Flowers mid-June–September. Small, silvery seed heads	3–5m (10–16½ft)
rehderiana	Straw-yellow with bright yellow stamens	Large panicles of small cowslip-like flowers, with a similar fragrance, July–September. Sunny position. From W. China twentieth century	6m (19½ft)
serratifolia	Pale lemon-yellow	Small flowers with a lemon scent, July–October, followed by attractive seed heads. From Korea at beginning twentieth century	4–5m (13–16½ft)

C. rehderiana needs a sunny position to produce its cowslip-like flowers

C. x triternata 'Rubro-marginata' has a dainty flower with a light, marzipan fragrance

Variety	Colour	Features	Height (approx.)
terniflora	White	Small, scented flowers with hosta-like leaves, August–September. Sunny position. Vigorous, from China and Japan	8m (26ft)
thunbergii	White with creamy-yellow stamens	Small, sweetly scented flowers with recurving sepals, in profusion, August–October	3–4m (10–13ft)
x triternata 'Rubro-marginata'	Bright mauve-pink fading to white at base	Masses of small flowers with a marzipan scent, July–September. Raised nineteenth century, *flammula* x *viticella*	3–4m (10–13ft)
veitchiana	Straw-yellow	A relative of *rehderiana*. Sweet scent. Plant in sun. From China early twentieth century	6m (19½ft)
viorna	Mauve-pink with cream inner	Nodding flowers, recurving sepals July–September. From east America, early eighteenth century	2–2.5m (6½–8ft)
virginiana	White with cream stamens	Small, sweetly scented flowers, large, deep bronze young leaves. August–October. From America mid-eighteenth century	4–5m (13–16½ft)
vitalba (Old Man's Beard)	Creamy-white, initially tinged green	Britain's native clematis. Flowers are followed by masses of seed heads. July–September	6–8m (19½–26ft)
'Western Virgin'	Pure white with yellow anthers	Small flowers in profusion, July–September. A vigorous hybrid, Canadian mid-twentieth century	11m (36ft)

CULTIVATION

PREPARATION

Planning

The most important prelude to planting is planning. How often have we bought impulsively only to find the colour or size of the plant does not fit into our scheme? We either live with our mistakes or we dig them out, feeling guilty and wasteful as we do so. With clematis it is especially important to plan and choose with care. The *montana* which looks quite insignificant in its pot at the garden centre can soon spread 6–9m (19½–29½ft), clambering over everything in its path – it is wonderful if you have the space for such a plant, but disastrous if not.

Choosing a site

It is important to select a site which suits the clematis you have in mind, because some will only flourish in warm, sheltered aspects whilst others grow happily on a north-facing wall. Clematis will not usually thrive in very shady locations, nor do they like exposed, windy conditions. They like their feet in the shade and their heads in the sun. With combination planting, the host plant can often provide the shade and shelter the clematis needs, but it will also compete for nourishment, and unless you compensate for this, the hungry clematis or the host plant will suffer.

Spiraea provides shelter for *Clematis* 'Arabella'

Clematis montana has plenty of room along this garden wall and provides a lovely backcloth for *Mimosa*

Suppliers

As the beauty and versatility of clematis becomes more widely appreciated and demand increases, so too does the opportunity to purchase from a wide variety of suppliers. Garden centres and nurseries are expanding their range and many DIY stores and supermarkets now stock popular varieties. Some of the lesser-known beauties are often only available from specialist growers and for the gardener who wishes to create striking combination planting, a visit to one of these special nurseries can be rewarding. Some specialist growers provide a mail-order service.

Choosing clematis

Most of the plants sold in pots are two or more years old. Inspect the plant thoroughly. Roots should be emerging through the drainage holes at the bottom. Most plants only

This plant has a good healthy root system

have one stem, but try to find one with strong buds low down and two stems. Pre-packed specimens are usually protected by fibrous material enclosed in plastic, making it difficult to inspect the root system. However, with careful planting and aftercare, many a chain store bargain can turn into a wonderful display at incredible value.

Plants in pots can be put into the ground at any time of the year as long as the soil is not frozen or waterlogged, but it is best done in spring or autumn when the soil is moist and they will not dry out too much. October is the ideal time, because the plant will have a chance to settle in and may well produce flowers the following year.

The soil

A vigorous and healthy plant producing a mass of lovely blooms for many years will reward the time and effort you bestow in providing the best conditions for it at the planting stage. Clematis do not appear to be fussy as to whether the soil is alkaline or acid, but they do need fertile, well-drained, humus-rich loam.

Shrub companions

If you intend the clematis to climb a shrub, choose a position where the clematis roots will be shaded for most of the day. Do not plant it too close, because the shrub may take the greater share of the moisture and nutrients from the soil. Also, clematis roots need lots of space in which to develop. Use a few canes, twigs or branches to train the clematis across to the shrub.

Into the trees

The ideal way to grow clematis up a tree is to plant them at the same time so that they grow together; this is how the rampant wild species around the world grow to such incredible heights. A little more work is required if you want to grow clematis up an existing tree. If you want flowers to decorate the trunk as well as the branches, the clematis will need some means of support; wire netting or a wire grid attached to the trunk is the best way to achieve this. The planting hole should be dug at least

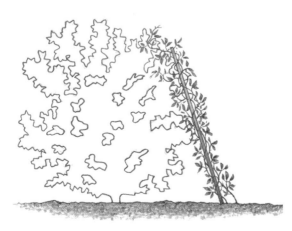

Planting a clematis so that it will grow into a shrub that is already well established.

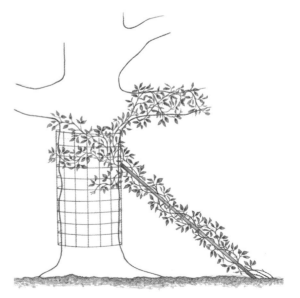

Planting a clematis so that it will grow up the trunk and into the branches of a tree

Wire mesh wrapped loosely around the trunk enables *macropetala* to climb up to the branches of the tree

60cm (2ft) away from the base of the tree and the clematis trained to it along a cane.

As an alternative, the clematis can be planted on the north side of the tree under the periphery of the branches and supported by stout canes or poles to reach them.

Fences and walls

When planting clematis to decorate the walls of a house or boundary, do not go too close to the structure; the soil there is often very dry because it has been shielded from the rain. Plant 60cm (2ft) away and train the clematis on canes or sticks towards the wall or fence. This method will help to prevent the clematis roots from becoming too dry.

Ground cover

When the climbing varieties of clematis are not provided with a means of support they will simply scramble over the soil as very attractive ground cover. This is an excellent way to view the open, saucer-shaped varieties. Without some means of support, however, it is very difficult to train them to cover a given

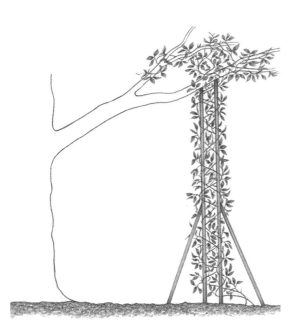

Planting directly under the branches is one way of getting clematis into the tree

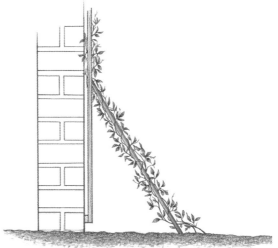

It is important to plant the clematis the correct distance from the wall so that it is not in the rain shadow

area. As they are blown about by the wind, they coil around their own stems in an effort to stablize themselves and in the end become quite entangled.

Wire mesh pegged down in the border can look wonderful when it is fully covered, but can be rather an eyesore in the early season when growth is new and then again later on when the leaves start to die.

A number of twigs pushed into the soil provides a more natural-looking support and you can add more as the clematis grows.

Low-growing shrubs are even more attractive as supports and the chapters on spring, summer and autumn provide a number of suggestions for combination planting.

PLANTING

Dig a hole that is at least 30cm (12in) across and 45cm (18in) deep. Fill the bottom 20cm (8in) with a planting mixture of one part fibrous, well-rotted compost, one part topsoil, and three handfuls of bonemeal for each barrow load.

Until recently the advice from nurserymen was to plant clematis 10cm (4in) below the surface to encourage the submerged buds to grow into new stems. This was an insurance against the existing stems developing stem rot (clematis wilt); more about this later. This method of deep planting can also provide protection during harsh winter conditions. New theories suggest that deep planting may be counterproductive in the endeavour to avoid stem rot, because it does not allow a free flow of air around the lower buds, thus allowing fungal spores to develop. Until more evidence has been accumulated, we can only presume that deep planting in cold areas will protect the roots and conventional planting in mild districts will enable free-flowing air. Whichever you choose, to encourage the production of new stems and strong growth every clematis should be pruned down to the lowest pair of healthy buds in the first February after planting. This will delay flowering on clematis that form flowers on the previous year's growth, but it is the most effective way of encouraging the production of new shoots and strong growth.

Before filling the hole, insert a feeding tube to aid watering and feeding of the root system. A two-litre plastic bottle with the base cut off,

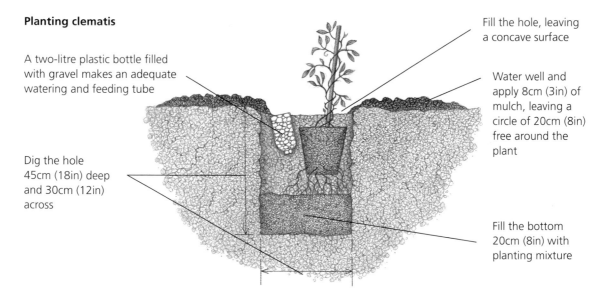

Planting clematis

A two-litre plastic bottle filled with gravel makes an adequate watering and feeding tube

Dig the hole 45cm (18in) deep and 30cm (12in) across

Fill the hole, leaving a concave surface

Water well and apply 8cm (3in) of mulch, leaving a circle of 20cm (8in) free around the plant

Fill the bottom 20cm (8in) with planting mixture

filled with gravel and placed into the hole, neck down, works well and usually lasts long enough for the plant to become deep rooted before the container finally perishes. Remember to remove the screw-on lid. A length of heavy-duty plastic tubing, the type used for downpipes, will provide a more permanent feeding tube.

Fill the hole with good-quality topsoil mixed with compost. Firm the soil around the plant, leaving a slightly concave surface, and water thoroughly. Then apply 8cm (3in) of mulching to keep the surface cool. Garden compost is ideal, or you can use mushroom compost, moist peat, leaf mould or bark. Leave a circle 20cm (8in) free of mulch around the plant to avoid rotting the stem, and check that the feeding tube is not covered.

SUPPORTS

There are three factors to consider when looking at ways to support clematis. First, there must be enough places for the clematis tendrils to wind, as they hate to feel insecure. Secondly, there should be a free flow of air around the plant to help prevent the onset of mildew. Thirdly, unless the clematis is of a type that is best grown in shade to protect its delicate colour, the root system should have a cool run but the flowers should be able to gravitate towards the sun.

Plants as supports
When growing clematis into host plants, as already stated they should be planted well away from their roots and trained towards their host on a cane. A few twisty ties will help to anchor it so that it does not get blown off course. Keep an eye out as it grows and continue to encourage it to stay with its partner; clematis are quite fickle and will happily wind themselves around foxgloves, delphiniums or any other nearby plant.

Trellis
Clematis cannot climb unless their tendrils have something to cling to; they are unable to grow on to a wall or fence without some additional means of support. They require a trellis or wires fashioned into a grid.

Wooden trellis is available in conventional square or diamond shapes and as they come in a range of different colours they can make attractive features in their own right. This is an important consideration for the winter months when the beautiful blooms are not there for decoration, especially so in the small garden where every feature needs to be carefully considered. Plastic-covered wire trellis is only suitable for small areas and is not as strong as wood. As the intention is for the clematis to stay for many years, it is worth investing in the strongest and most attractive means of support within your budget.

Air should be allowed to flow freely around the clematis and this will not be the case if the trellis is fixed directly on to the wall or fence; it needs to be proud. This can be achieved by

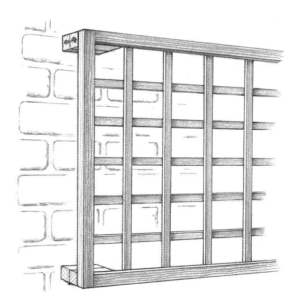

A hinged trellis can be lowered from the wall for any necessary maintenance

Wire netting has been fixed to the roof of this outbuilding to encourage a rampant *montana* to cover it completely

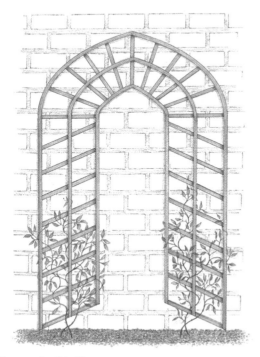

Trompe l'oeil trellis

first fixing wooden battens on to the wall and then screwing the trellis on to these. If you also fix corresponding battens on to the trellis, the bottom pair can be hinged together and the top pair fixed with hooks and eyes, thus allowing the whole thing to be unhooked and lowered to the ground. This allows easy access to the wall or fence for decorating or fresh preservative to be applied to the trellis.

Trellis can also be purchased in *trompe-l'oeil* style and when placed on a wall will create the illusion of an archway. The effect can be further enhanced by painting the centre of the archway in a different colour from the surrounding wall or by filling it with mirrored glass. The latter is ideal for a small courtyard garden where it will create the illusion of space as it reflects plants and light.

Clematis will look very effective growing around the outer archway, but do not choose a rampant variety or the effect will be lost.

A strong wire grid provides excellent support for climbers on this large boundary wall

Vine eyes and wire

Whilst it may not look quite as attractive as wooden trellis, strong wire threaded between vine eyes – screws with a loop at the end – provides an inexpensive and effective alternative. The wires should be spaced approximately 30cm (12in) apart horizontally and vertically thus creating a square grid. Brick and concrete walls will need to be drilled and plugged to hold the vine eyes. Buy the longest ones you can so that the wire is held away from the wall, thus allowing air to circulate freely around the plant.

Pergolas and arbours

A pergola over a pathway or an arbour in a secluded part of the garden, where you can sit peacefully and while away an hour or two, not only make lovely features but also provide an opportunity to grow clematis and other climbing plants.

C. viticella 'Margot Koster' has been trained to cover the upright of this pergola at RHS Rosemoor Garden

A rose trained along a rope between the uprights of a pergola provides a very attractive feature

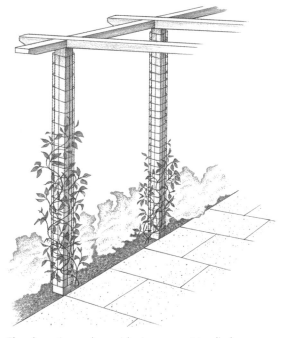

The clematis needs a grid wire support to climb over the pergola successfully

When planning a pergola or arbour, ensure that it is both high and wide enough to allow you to walk or sit beneath it without brushing against the plants. This is especially important when growing roses because their thorns can be quite painful. If the plan is to grow roses and clematis together, the rose should be trained around the upright; it will then provide a natural support for the clematis. Encourage the clematis to twine around the lower branches, otherwise it will bolt straight up.

Clematis grown on their own or with other less woody climbers will need other means of support if they are to climb the poles. Strands of wire wrapped around and tacked into place are not really adequate unless you are prepared to spend time tying the new growth to them regularly. Plastic-coated wire trellis provides more support, bends quite easily and can be stapled or nailed into position. Square grid wire netting is another option.

Wooden trellis can be fixed between the uprights of an arbour to provide support for plants as they spread and a little three-sided house of plants like this looks wonderful when covered with sweet-smelling climbers and a mass of clematis blooms.

Roses can be trained to spread along a heavy-duty rope that is fixed between the uprights of a pergola and clematis will often follow them.

Free-standing supports

Obelisks and tripods can be used to great effect in the border and on the patio. Tripods can be placed in large tubs or barrels to provide support for the smaller varieties of clematis. They can be purchased in wood and wrought iron, the latter being elegant if somewhat expensive.

A simple framework to set in a border can be made out of three rustic poles 1.8–2.1m (6–7ft) long, set in a triangle. Nine crossbars

Clematis 'Mrs Cholmondley', beautifully supported on a simple rustic structure at the British Clematis Society Gardens, Bourne Hall, Surrey

A three-sided support made from rustic poles and covered with a clematis makes an attractive feature in the border

can be made out of the same type of poles sawn in half. One pole should provide six crossbars of 60cm (24in) in length. A timber merchant will usually cut them to size ready for you to nail or screw together. Simple free-standing structures such as this can be used very effectively to create height in areas where it is lacking.

Another simple and very effective support can be made by placing a 2m (6½ft) fence post into a Met post inserted into the ground, or by simply cementing the post into the ground. The post should be 1.8m (6ft) above ground level. Encase the post in a column made of four pieces of 30cm x 1.8m (1 x 6ft) trellis nailed together. Then screw or nail the trellis to the post in one corner.

Bean and pea supports in the shape of a wigwam can now be purchased and at the end

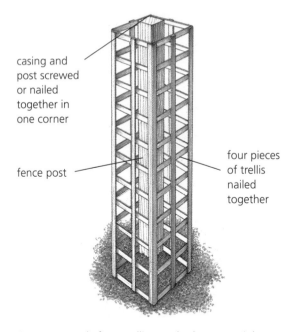

casing and post screwed or nailed together in one corner

fence post

four pieces of trellis nailed together

A support made from trellis attached to an upright post secured in the ground

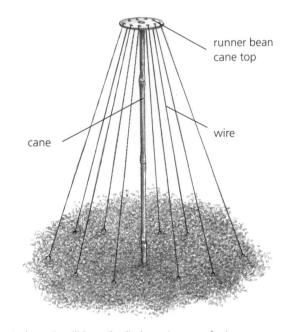

runner bean cane top

cane

wire

A clematis will happily climb a wigwam of wires suspended from a bean pole

of the season they can be lifted and stored in the shed for the winter months. A support such as this is quite adequate for one or two small clematis, especially those varieties that are hard pruned annually, because the support can be put back in place before the growing season starts.

A very similar structure can be made with a 2.1m (7ft) cane. Push the cane into the ground. Slip a runner bean cane top over the end of the cane and attach strong, plastic-coated wire to the holes. Tie the ends of the wires to tent pegs and push these firmly into the ground to create a circle. The result should look like a maypole before the dancing begins.

AFTERCARE

Watering and feeding

Clematis are very hungry and thirsty plants. A feeding tube will help to get water and nourishment to the root system. Water regularly, especially during the first season when the roots are becoming established. In very dry weather, 5 litres (1 gallon) per plant each day is not excessive.

Feed weekly during the growing season with a liquid fertilizer high in potash diluted to the manufacturer's recommendations. Do not give liquid fertilizer when the clematis is in bloom as this will shorten the flowering period, but do continue with the watering programme. A handful of bonemeal around each plant in the autumn, gently worked into the soil, will provide a slow-release fertilizer to encourage root growth. This is also a good time to top up the mulching.

Pruning

The two things that are likely to deter people from buying clematis are 'clematis wilt', which we will cover later, and the perceived difficulties related to pruning.

Whilst it is not quite as simple as 'bloom before June, no need to prune', if you have inherited a number of clematis and do not even know their names let alone their pruning requirements, you will not go far wrong if you live by this maxim. It would seem that the earlier clematis come into flower, the less pruning they need, but pruning clematis and training them in accordance with their needs is essential if we are to enjoy them at their best. All too often we see clematis growing on one stem with their flowers in a cluster above eye level. What we want to achieve is a healthy plant with a number of shoots and flowers from the bottom to the top.

The first step towards achieving this goal is to hard prune *all* clematis in the first February after planting. This will encourage the plant to grow another stem. During spring, as the stems are growing, pinch some of them out to encourage fan-shaped growth.

For pruning purposes, the different kinds of clematis can be divided into three categories:

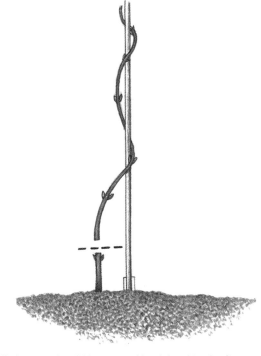

All clematis should be pruned back hard in the first February after planting

Category 1

No pruning required. Flowers are formed on the previous year's growth. Clematis groups in this category are the *cirrhosa*, *armandii*, *alpina*, *macropetala* and *montana*.

Note: If any of the clematis in this category becomes too entangled and overgrown, they can be cut back to a more manageable level after flowering. If the stems are really thick and old, the plant may not recover from the shock if too much is removed at once; it is preferable to tackle the job over two or three seasons.

Category 2

Light pruning. Flowers are formed on the previous year's growth. In February, work your way down from the top of each stem to a plump and healthy bud. Prune just above it. Clematis groups in this category are the early and mid-season large-flowered varieties.

Note: The early varieties usually commence flowering in May and June with a second flush in September. If you prune them too heavily you will be short of early flowers. If the blooms are all at the top with few lower down and the clematis has a healthy number of stems, after flowering prune back some of the stems to encourage new growth.

Mid-season varieties usually commence flowering in June and continue right through to September. Here there is the choice of light pruning or hard pruning. Once again a mixture of both will ensure new growth that can be trained to bear flowers low down.

Category 3

Hard pruning. Flowers are formed on the current year's growth. In February, from the bottom of the plant and on every stem, work up to a pair of healthy buds and cut just above them. Clematis groups in this category are the late, large-flowered hybrids, *viticellas*, *orientalis*, *texensis* and herbaceous varieties.

Light pruning for clematis that bear flowers on the previous year's growth

Hard pruning for clematis that bear flowers on the current year's growth

Note: Clematis of the *orientalis* family can look very effective when grown through large shrubs and small trees, in which case cut back some of the stems in February to encourage new growth and leave others to continue their climb. There may come a point after a few years when a complete hard pruning is required.

Holiday care

Once a good root system has been established, the plant can draw from a deeper level where moisture is retained for a longer period. Thorough watering of the surrounding area and a good thick mulching will probably suffice for the duration of most holidays.

Young plants in their first season may suffer badly, especially during a period of drought. If possible, arrange for someone to water the plants regularly during your absence. A reciprocal arrangement with a fellow gardener can work well and often develops a shared interest in each other's gardens.

For people who have to leave their gardens unattended frequently, there are sophisticated watering systems available that work on a timed device. The reward of returning home to a glorious display of clematis may well justify such an investment.

Labelling

As your collection of clematis grows, the importance of labelling will become evident. In early spring, when faced with pruning plants in close proximity, often tangled into one another and with no distinctive flowers as a guide, your memory can let you down. Label the plant immediately after planting, tying or staking. Add a pruning code and attach the label to the base of the plant.

Pruning code 1: No need to prune (except to tidy and control growth)

Pruning code 2: Prune lightly (each stem, two buds down from the top)

Pruning code 3: Prune severely (each stem, two buds up from the base)

There are a number of types of labels on the market. Opt for those that are durable and attractive and use a marker pen. There is nothing more irritating than trying to read faded, worn-out labels and it could lead to incorrect pruning. Check the labels periodically and renew or re-write them when necessary.

A planting plan, regularly updated will prove invaluable when planning a pruning schedule for clematis and their host plants.

Transplanting

There are a number of reasons why you may need to move an established clematis: garden re-design, clashing colours, plant not able to be shown to best advantage, overcrowding, and so on. Take heart, it can be done, although it must be stated that clematis are very individual plants and some sulk more than others at being moved. On the whole, the hardier the clematis the better the success rate. Spring is the best time to undertake the operation, as this will give the plant time to recover during the growing season.

Clematis of the pruning code 3 varieties should be pruned down to two nodes (leaf joints) from the base of the plant. Others will need to be pruned as severely as possible without cutting too much into the thick woody stems. Dig out the plant with as much root ball and soil as possible and, unless you have a ready-prepared hole, wrap the root ball in a bag or sheet of heavy-duty plastic into which drainage holes have been punched and tie it up. Plant it as soon as possible. If there is going to be an extended delay, wrap the root ball in hessian and store it in a sheltered part of the garden. Ensure that the plant is kept

If a lifted clematis is not to be replanted immediately, wrap the root ball in hessian to keep it moist

moist but not waterlogged. After replanting, pay particular attention to feeding and watering for the next six months and the plant should recover. It is not unusual for a small piece of root to be left behind from which a new plant develops.

GROWING CLEMATIS IN CONTAINERS

Container gardening has become increasingly popular as people extend their homes into the garden with smartly dressed terraces and patios. For the small garden, pots and tubs are invaluable, because they can be planted with the best of the current season's offerings and simply placed wherever they will make the most impact. Many gardeners are now seeking unusual plants and combinations to enhance the lovely containers that are available in an ever-increasing variety of materials, shapes and colours.

It is still quite rare to see clematis grown in containers. This may be due to disappointing experiences or because of the time and effort required to grow them successfully in this way. However, if you are prepared to choose the container and clematis wisely, plant carefully and meet the extra feeding and watering requirements, there is no doubt that clematis in containers on the patio or in a courtyard garden can be very effective indeed. They can take colour to a higher level or tumble down in a rippling sheet of colour.

Containers also provide an opportunity to grow clematis of a more tender variety, because they can be moved into a frost-free area for the winter.

Types of containers

Many disappointing results are experienced due to planting clematis in containers that are too small. This is quite understandable, because it is not easy to find containers that are as large as 45cm (18in) deep with a 30cm (12in) diameter, but this is the ideal size in which to grow one or possibly two small clematis. Large wooden half barrels and Versailles-style planters generally fall short of the required depth, but usually compensate by having a larger diameter. If you are handy at do-it-yourself or 'know a man who can', you can make a wooden container 45cm (18in) deep and 45cm (18in) square in which to grow two or more clematis and a few supporting plants, or a shrub over which the clematis can tumble.

Very large terracotta pots look attractive, but make sure that they are frost hardy. Ali Baba shapes also look very attractive but are not practical because it is hard to replace the top soil annually and even more difficult to remove the plant without damaging it when you need to replace the soil completely.

PREPARING, PLANTING AND MAINTAINING CONTAINERS

❦ When buying clematis, choose varieties that are suitable for growing in containers. For example, containers are not suitable for the very rampant varieties.

❦ Wooden containers should be treated with a safe proprietary preservative before planting commences.

❦ Line the sides, but not the bottom, of the container with insulating material; this will help to keep the roots cool in summer and warm in winter. One way is to line it with tin foil, shiny side to the container, and then add a 10cm (1in) layer of newspaper; another is to use heavy-duty plastic or bubble wrap.

❦ Make sure there are sufficient drainage holes or the plant will become waterlogged.

❦ Site the container in the required position. Ensure that the aspect suits the chosen clematis and companion plants if there are any. Use bricks, blocks or battens to raise the container off the ground to assist free drainage.

❦ Place a good layer of broken pots, stones or pebbles into the base of the container, again to aid drainage.

❦ Mix together half quantity of fertile friable soil with half compost, or use a commerical soil-based compost such as John Innes No. 2. Add two handfuls of bonemeal and a tablespoonful of general fertilizer such as Growmore and fill the container to within 5cm (2in) of the rim.

❦ The clematis will need support if it is to climb. There are special metal or wooden obelisks available from suppliers that look very attractive. If these are beyond your budget, insert three or more canes around the diameter of the container and tie them at the top in a wigwam style or fan them out. Alternatively, place the container against a wall or fence on to which trellis has been fixed. The clematis is then simply trained from the container to the trellis.

❦ Plant the clematis deeply to encourage new shoots to form.

❦ Water the container thoroughly and finish off with 5cm (2in) layer of small pebbles or bark to retain moisture.

❦ Water regularly, once daily during the growing season, twice daily during hot and dry conditions. Never allow the container to become dry at any time of year. If the surface is dry for a depth of 1–2cm (1–1¾in), water is needed. Do not over-water clematis; the soil should be moist all through, but not sodden or nutrients will be washed away and the roots become over-saturated.

❦ Feed the clematis regularly during the growing season with a potash-based fertilizer, but stop as soon as the flowers begin to open or their season will be shortened. If the clematis is of a variety that blooms in the early summer and again later, feed between flushes to encourage a heavier crop of flowers.

Lining provides valuable insulation in a container

Stone containers of the required size are prohibitively expensive but will last virtually forever and make a superb, permanent feature. There are also concrete look-a-likes but unfortunately, and despite new and vastly improved technology, they never quite meet the visual impact of the real thing. Nonetheless they make a good, sturdy, long-lasting alternative. The problem with both of these materials is their weight. They are virtually impossible to move once filled.

There has been a vast improvement recently in the quality of plastic containers, which come in all shapes, sizes and finishes. The advantage of plastic is that it is light and has good insulating properties.

Select your container with care if you want to grow clematis successfully. Think big.

PESTS AND DISEASES

There is a quite a lot of literature available on the subject of controlling pests and diseases and gardeners today are becoming increasingly aware of the need to preserve an ecological balance which cannot always be maintained with an excessive use of chemicals. There are a number of pests and diseases that will attack clematis and here we look at some of the ways to control them by chemical and organic methods.

Health and safety is a serious issue for the gardener, especially when using chemicals. When spraying or dusting, do so in calm weather conditions. It is wise to protect your eyes and mouth. To avoid spraying, systemic insecticides and fungicides can be watered into the surrounding soil; the roots absorb and distribute the chemical up through the rest of the plant. If possible, avoid spraying plants when they are in flower, because certain chemicals can affect bees and hoverflies. If you must spray, do so at dusk when the insects have finished collecting pollen and nectar.

Hoverflies feed on pollen and nectar. A hoverfly larva eats over a thousand aphids during its development

Slugs and snails

These molluscs love clematis, especially those that are young and tender. They can strip a stem and eat young shoots until the plant is decimated or is so weakened that it is vulnerable to disease and adverse weather conditions. Their presence can usually be identified by the slimy trail they leave behind. Slugs are persistent clematis diners all year round. Snails hibernate in the cold weather but are by far the greater climbers; they can scale a wall to incredible heights. Unfortunately, they are both so numerous and so persistent that it is virtually impossible to win the battle against them. Do try to keep them at bay when new, young growth emerges to give the plant a chance to develop a thick, woody stem that is not so easily stripped.

The only really effective deterrent is slug bait, usually sold as pellets which should be applied in accordance with the manufacturer's instructions. Regular removal of the carcasses will help to prevent them being eaten by other wildlife. Birds and hedgehogs are especially vulnerable. There are little black plastic containers on the market known as 'slug hotels' in which the bait is placed and the slugs die, supposedly out of the reach of other animals and birds.

There are more ecologically friendly methods that can be tried. A circle of stones around the plant coated in Vaseline can create a slippery barrier which is difficult for slugs and snails to climb. Equally a barrier of sharp gravel, bark or crushed eggshells may deter them. Ground up coconut shells are considered to be very effective. Many gardeners place a container of beer nearby to which the pests are attracted and drown in a blissful state. However, this may not be until they have dined on a first course of tender young clematis shoots. Unfortunately, it can also be a trap for beneficial wildlife, such as beetles and worms.

Earwigs

Yellow-brown insects 2cm (¾in) long, easily recognized by the pair of pincers that protrude from the front of their heads. Earwigs are voracious eaters especially towards the end of the summer season when they can decimate flowers, buds and foliage. They hide during the day and feed at night. By placing an inverted flowerpot, loosely stuffed with straw, on to a cane near the clematis plants, you will create a daytime shelter for them from which they can removed and disposed of. Alternatively, dust the plants with HCH (Lindane) powder or permethrin.

A flowerpot stuffed with straw provides a daytime refuge for earwigs. They can then be disposed of before they start their nightly forage for food

Clematis 'Huldine' has provided a tasty snack for something. The shape of the holes would indicate that earwigs were the culprits

Aphids

Aphids are sometimes attracted to young plants. There are a number of insecticides available to control them. Pirimicard is both selective and systemic, thus leaving animals, birds and beneficial insects unharmed. Many birds and insects feed on aphids and by attracting these friendly predators to your garden you may alleviate or at least minimize the need for chemical control.

Vine weevil

The adult vine weevil, a greyish-black beetle 9mm (⅜in) long, has a short snout and antennae and like the earwig feeds nightly on foliage. Their presence can be identified by notches appearing on leaf margins often near the base of the plant. Control is difficult. They do not appear to be attracted like the earwig to a home of straw in an inverted pot, preferring to hide nearer ground level in plant debris. The removal of dead and rotting plant growth is probably the best deterrent. In serious cases, spray at dusk with HCH, permethrin or pirimiphos-methyl.

Vine weevils cause more serious damage at the larvae stage. Adults deposit their eggs near the roots of plants such as clematis, where they develop into white plump larvae 1cm (½in) long that feed on stems underground. Their presence is not usually known until the plant becomes sick. Weevils consider plants in pots in the greenhouse to be the perfect nursery for egg deposits. Once again, good hygiene will help to deter the adult from finding a resting place. Drenching the plants with HCH or pirimiphos-methyl in mid-summer with a follow-up treatment one month later, can kill young larvae.

Clematis wilt

The major dread of the clematis grower is stem rot, commonly known as 'clematis wilt'. One day the plant looks bright and healthy, the next it begins to look droopy and sad. Within a week the leaves turn brown and then black, the flowers shrivel and die and to all intents and purposes the plant looks as if it completely dead.

Research into the cause of clematis wilt has not yet been fully conclusive, but it suggests that a fungus called *Ascochyta clemcidina* plays a major role. It tends to attack young, green stems of plants in their early years. It works across the stem cutting off the supply of sap to the plant.

The good news is that the plant below the affected area, which is often at a node close to ground level, is invariably unaffected. So the remedy is to cut off the stem below the affected node, continue with a good watering and feeding programme and with luck new shoots will soon appear. Sometimes only a single stem is affected and the others remain in good health.

Caution is required, however, before cutting down a plant so severely. Many a wilting clematis may only be doing so because it is thirsty. Water well; if it does not recover by the next day, stem rot may well be the cause and action will be required. Make sure that all affected debris is burnt to prevent the spread of the disease.

So far, investigations have shown that the large-flowered clematis with an ancestry of *Clematis lanuginosa* is especially susceptible to fungal stem rot. Unfortunately, some of the finest large-flowered clematis have this parentage and it would be a great shame if we were never to grow such beauties as 'Mrs. Cholmondley', 'Vyvyan Pennel' or 'Mrs. N. Thompson', to name but a few. So what can be done to help prevent fungal stem rot?

The most important factor is the gardener's ability to exercise patience. When planting any clematis, especially those that are more susceptible to the disease, follow the planting and pruning recommendations to encourage strong and plentiful stems. In some cases, a plant can be affected by fungal stem rot a number of times. Should this be the case, do not be in a hurry to abandon it. Follow the procedure of cutting down the affected stems, watering and feeding until the plant reaches maturity with some nice woody stems that are too hard for the fungus to attack.

This 'Gypsy Queen' is covered in the white powdery substance known as 'mildew'

Fungicides can be sprayed or watered into the surrounding soil in spring and again in autumn to help prevent stem rot, but it is recommended that a variety of types is used throughout the season, such as Bordeaux mixture, liquid copper and benomyl, to deter the fungus from developing immunity.

Clematis growers have made great strides in developing new cultivars and hybrids that are resistant to stem rot and eventually this disease may be a thing of the past. For now, for the gardener who wishes to avoid the risk, there is a wide choice of plants available with a proven history of resistance to disease, especially amongst the small-flowered varieties.

Mildew

A white, powdery substance appears on the leaves, often attacking plants later in the season, causing the leaves to turn yellow and fall. It can completely disfigure the plant at a time when the flowers could still be giving a lovely display. The major cause of mildew is fungi thriving on plants in dry conditions. It is spread by wind and rain splashes. At the first sign of attack, immediately remove and burn the affected growth. If the condition persists, treat it with a suitable fungicide. To help prevent mildew, ensure that the clematis is well watered and apply a good depth of mulching to preserve moisture during a time of drought.

INCREASING STOCK

For the amateur gardener, the three easiest ways to increase his or her stock of clematis is to grow them from seeds, to take cuttings or by layering.

Growing from seeds

Plants grown from the seeds of species clematis will probably turn out to be very similar to the parent plant. Plants grown from hybrid

GROWING CLEMATIS FROM SEED

Sowing the seed

❧ Use 10cm (4in) pots or small seed trays that are not too shallow, because clematis form long roots quite quickly. Fill the pots to within 1cm (½in) of the top with moist, well-drained, soil-based seed compost. Firm the surface lightly.

❧ Sow the seed evenly. Do not overcrowd. There is no need to remove the fluff from the seed. Sieve a little more compost on top, just to cover the seeds, and add 5mm (¼in) of very coarse sand or grit, which will help to protect the seeds from disturbance.

❧ Stand the pot in water containing a fungicide until the grit shows signs of dampness.

❧ Label clearly with name and date, and place the pots outside or in a cold greenhouse in a well-lit position out of direct sunlight. If they are to be placed outside, protect them from birds, mice and so on by covering them with a sheet of glass or plastic.

❧ Check periodically to make sure the compost is moist but not saturated.

❧ Most clematis will germinate without heat, in fact many varieties seem to need a cold period prior to germination. Germination may be erratic; they may come all at once or be spread out over several months.

Potting on

❧ It is best to let the seedlings reach a height of about 5cm (2in) before transplanting them. Late summer is a good time, but if they are not large enough by the autumn, leave them until the following spring.

❧ Make sure the pot or tray of seedlings is well watered before transplanting them into individual pots no smaller than 6.5cm (2½in) deep and containing seed compost. Handle the seedlings gently, holding them by their leaves.

❧ Tall seedlings can be pinched back. Pinching back should be carried out at each re-potting stage.

❧ Label each pot with the plant's name.

❧ Lastly, stand the pot in a sheltered spot in the open garden or in a cold greenhouse, away from direct sunlight.

Species plants such as this *Clematis macropetala* are more likely to reproduce true to type than hybrids and cultivares

clematis or any of the large-flowered cultivars may turn out to be very different from their parents in size, shape, colour and vigour. You may produce a wonderful new variety or a rather worthless plant. The seeds of species plants seem to be easier to germinate and if conditions are right you may see the first little shoot in about six weeks. The seeds of large-flowered hybrids may take very much longer to germinate. Spring is a good time to sow seeds. With luck you may have some seedlings ready to transplant in the summer.

Growing plants from cuttings

An inter-nodal softwood cutting is the recommended method for clematis. The best time is mid-spring or early summer.

GROWING CLEMATIS FROM CUTTINGS

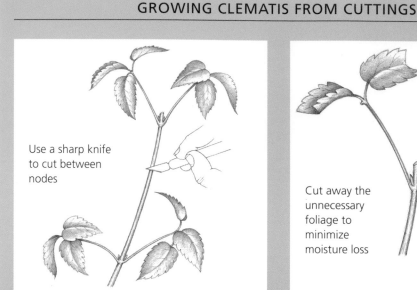

Use a sharp knife to cut between nodes

Cut away the unnecessary foliage to minimize moisture loss

❦ Prepare the pots by ensuring they are thoroughly clean. Fill to within 1cm (½in) of the top with cutting compost. Firm lightly. Add a top layer of coarse sand or grit.

❦ Cut a length of vine from the mid section which is neither too soft nor too woody.

❦ With a clean sharp blade, cut through the vine immediately above a node and again about 4cm (1½in) below the same node.

❦ Reduce the foliage by removing all leaves from one side and cutting any large remaining leaves in half. This will help to reduce moisture loss until the cuttings have rooted.

❦ Completely immerse the prepared cuttings in a fungicide mixture. Allow them to drain.

❦ Dip the base of the cutting into rooting powder and shake off any excess.

❦ Make holes in the compost with a dibber or pencil and insert the cuttings around the pot. Do not overcrowd; the foliage should not be touching. The node should be level with the grit or coarse sand.

❦ Attach a label and water the pots with fungicide diluted to the manufacturer's recommendation; use a fine spray.

❦ Place the pots in a propagator or cover them with polythene to create a humid atmosphere. A temperature of 20°C (68°F) will aid rooting which should take place in four weeks. Check by gently pulling on a leaf. If it feels firm, the cutting will probably have formed roots.

❦ Pot the cuttings separately or at least make sure that they are not touching. Grow the plants on for another year before setting them in the garden. Nip the side shoots periodically to encourage strong growth.

A number of cuttings in one pot

SERPENTINE LAYERING

❦ First, prepare the soil next to the parent plant. The soil should be fertile and friable. If compost is added it should be done three or four weeks beforehand.

❦ Carefully bend a trailing shoot down to the prepared soil. Trim off the leaves and the side shoots.

❦ At suitable intervals along the stem, close to the nodes, make several small cuts (not all the way through the stem). Brush these wounds with hormone powder.

❦ Peg down the wounded sections using U-shaped pieces of wire.

❦ Separate the plantlets in autumn, by which time the roots should have formed.

❦ Trim away the old stem and put the new plant into a 13cm (5in) pot of soil-based potting compost.

❦ Grow on until the plant is well established, nipping it back periodically to encourage strong new growth.

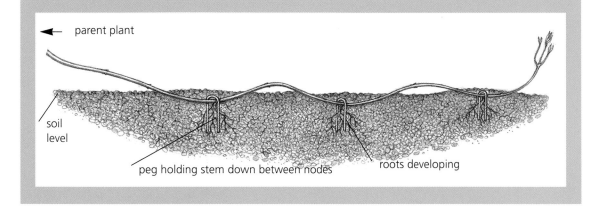

parent plant

soil level

peg holding stem down between nodes

roots developing

Layering

One of the easiest and most reliable ways of increasing stock is by layering. Clematis usually responds well to this method and when layered in spring will be rooted by autumn.

Layering is undertaken in the bed alongside the parent plant. Because clematis stems are so pliable, a number of plantlets can be produced from a single stem. This is known as 'serpentine layering'.

3

PARTNERS
FOR SPRING

March winds will blow
and we will have snow,
and what will the robin
do then, poor thing?
He'll sit in a barn
and keep himself warm,
and hide his head under
his wing, poor thing.

L IKE the robin, the gardener may well wish to hide away in the barn, or the potting shed, frustrated that spring's promise of longer, warmer days is not being fulfilled. February's snowdrops were bright and cheery, pushing their way through even the hardest and coldest of soil and appearing positively to revel in the snow.

C. cirrhosa 'Wisley Cream' does not require pruning unless it becomes too rampant

The crocuses also seem to be undeterred and look their best when planted in drifts around the garden. The golden daffodils of March are a sign that spring has finally arrived but even they look a bit despondent when battered by winds or covered in ice and snow. A calm, sunny March day, with a feeling of warmth in the air, may be rare but it is all that a gardener needs to get outside with renewed vigour and tackle the jobs that will help him or her to accomplish the wonderful ideas that he or she has planned for the coming year.

Cold March winds bring a chill that masks the slight warming of the season and it is often a revelation, when walking around the garden in early spring, to find how much movement there is, with buds forming and shoots emerging. Indeed, it is already a bit late to be pruning clematis, for they will have started to make new growth.

Pruning time

February is the ideal time to prune clematis that need it, and the extra expense and effort you made to label your clematis with their pruning codes will be rewarded as you face your collection of bare, twisted stems that all appear to be the same. Whilst these pruning codes are invaluable, there is no substitute for getting to know the pruning needs of the various clematis groups and thinking about what you would like each individual plant to achieve in its particular location.

You may have an *orientalis* or a large-flowered mid-season hybrid that blooms continuously from June to September. With these varieties you have the choice of pruning hard, pruning partially or not at all. Much will depend upon where they are growing. If they are on a tripod or in a container, you may wish to prune them quite hard. If however, they are happily scrambling up a tree or large shrub they can either be left to get on with it or pruned partially to encourage flowers to form on the lower stems.

Choosing clematis

For those living in warmer climate zones who have been able to accommodate the evergreen *Clematis cirrhosa*, their cream, bell-shaped flowers will have cheered your winter.

You may also be fortunate enough to have space on a warm, sheltered wall for a rampant *Clematis armandii* with its large, evergreen leaves and sweetly scented, white flowers that appear in March.

If your climate is too harsh for such luxuries, you will have to wait a few more weeks before hardy *Clematis macropetala* with her pretty, double, tutu-shaped flowers arrives in April joined by the equally hardy *Clematis alpina*, which is very similar in appearance and habit. If space is at a premium, these lovely early clematis are an excellent choice being quite easily contained.

Clematis montana needs a lot more space, but why not cover your shed, fence, or house wall with one and revel in the mass of white or pink flowers that waft their delicate scent on a warm day in May? After the blooms, you will be left with a luxuriant growth of attractive leaves.

Early, large-flowered hybrids also start appearing in May. Big and exotic, in a breathtaking range of colours, they are hard to resist. This is by far the largest clematis group and you will be spoilt for choice. You can use your trees, shrubs and roses as companions to a small collection. Visit your local garden centre in late spring and you will probably see a good selection of container-grown plants in flower. Do not forget to read the label for height and preferred location before you make a purchase to ensure it will suit the home you have in mind for it.

Timely tasks

Clematis need plenty of water at all times, so when it doesn't rain for a few days remember your watering can. They will especially appreciate being fed during their growing season, but once they flower it is best to stop feeding to slow down the growing process. That way you will be able to enjoy the flowers for a much longer period.

If worms have not already completed the job, now is the time to fork in what remains of last year's mulch, together with a handful or two of bonemeal to act as a slow-release fertilizer. While the soil is still damp, apply a new good depth of mulch to help preserve moisture and provide a cool root run.

Tie in the stems of climbing varieties before they go off track or they will wrap their tenacious tendrils where they are not welcome: prize tulips, wallflowers, the washing line – they do not mind as long as they feel secure. Handle them gently because their tender new stems can easily break. Snails and slugs love these tender shoots too and will decimate these stems as they emerge from the ground unless you do something about it.

The peeling bark of *Betula paprifera* provides a focal point in winter and early spring

Spring is a busy time for the gardener. You may feel daunted by the jobs that caring for clematis adds to your schedule, especially if gardening has to be squeezed in between the demands of children, a full-time job and indoor do-it-yourself projects. If you can give some time to these tasks, you will definitely reap the benefit of a succession of lovely clematis to enjoy all year round. If you really have little time to spare, go for *alpina*, *macropetala* and *montana*, which you can enjoy in the spring; they are hardy and quite independent and, unless it is an exceptionally dry spring, will forgive the neglect that may daunt the large hybrids.

EARLY SPRING

Evergreen clematis

Winter and early spring is the time to review whether the structural planting in the garden is working well. At this time of year, in northern climates, the garden is mostly viewed from the comfort of the house, so it is pleasing if each vista presents an individual experience. Perhaps one window looks out on to a pond or small water feature where plants reflect in the water and birds come to drink. The eye may be drawn through another window to a tree, such as *Prunus serrula* (cherry), whose copper-coloured bark glistens in the spring sunshine, or the ghostly glow of *Betula* (silver birch) whose white branches and bark shine despite the cloud and gloom. Evergreen shrubs, a clump of *hellebores* (Christmas rose) and early spring bulbs all help to create eye-catching features.

In cold and dismal weather, it often takes something very special to draw us outside: perhaps the glimpse of a flower that we would like to see more closely. If the flower emits a pleasant perfume, invariably we reach out to hold it close to receive the full impact and we are in touch with nature and our garden again.

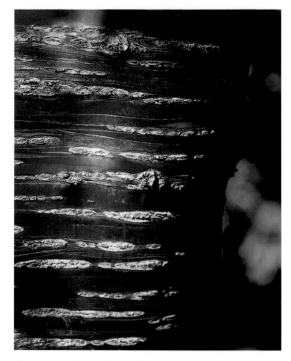

The copper-brown bark of *Prunus serrula* glows in the early spring sunshine

Clematis of the *cirrhosa* and *armandii* groups fulfil these requirements admirably with their pretty flowers that emit a gentle fragrance and their evergreen leaves. The only drawback is that they are not fully frost hardy, although they have been grown quite successfully in the southern counties of Britain and even in more northerly districts where appropriate shelter has been provided.

The family of *C. cirrhosa* blooms from November to March and has finely cut, evergreen leaves that are slightly bronzed underneath. The flowers are cream, open cup-shaped, with some varieties having red flecks. The *C. armandii* group has larger and thicker dark green, glossy leaves that are a most attractive light bronze when young. The sweetly scented white, saucer-shaped flowers are borne in March and April. *C. armandii* makes an impressive sight when grown to its full potential because it can reach 5m (16½ft)

Acacia is even more frost tender than the evergreen *Clematis indivisa*. Both grow beautifully together at the RHS garden Rosemoor in north Devon

quite easily when it is happy in its environment. Unfortunately, if caught by extreme cold and frost, it does tend to droop and look sorry for itself. It seems to appreciate the company of other wall shrubs, such as *Ceanothus* or quince, on to which it can wrap its tendrils securely and thus protect its large leaves from excessive wind damage.

Pruning evergreen clematis is not essential, but if you wish to keep them in check – because they are quite rampant – do so immediately after they have finished flowering so that they have the opportunity to grow new stems for next year's flowers.

If you can provide a warm, sheltered wall, lovely partnerships can be formed between evergreen clematis and other frost-tender trees and shrubs. *Acacia* (mimosa), native to warm, temperate regions of the globe, is frost tender

and can only be grown outdoors in mild climate zones. Of the acacia varieties *baileyana* is a small, graceful tree of 5m (16½ft), *dealbata* is a larger tree reaching 10m (33ft) or more, and *podalyriifolia* is a medium-sized shrub and a more manageable size for a small garden, although its leaves are not quite as attractive. Mimosa's small, yellow, sweetly scented flowers, borne in racemes or panicles, look quite spectacular in late winter/early spring, especially when partnered with evergreen *C. indivisa* whose pure white flowers and yellow stamens harmonize beautifully with the mimosa blossoms. Mimosa and *indivisa* are both ideal conservatory plants where their fragrances will combine to create a heady perfume. When planting inside, use a very large container filled with a neutral or acid, loam-based potting compost, water freely

Pittosporum, an attractive evergreen shrub, makes an ideal companion for early-flowering, evergreen *Clematis foresti*, seen here at RHS Rosemoor

during the growing season and apply a balanced liquid fertilizer monthly. Outdoor planting requires an acid or neutral soil against a sunny, south-facing wall.

Pittosporum is another genus of frost-tender shrubs and trees. The variety *tenuifolium*, with its wavy-margined, glossy, evergreen leaves, can withstand a short period below 0°C (32°F). This lovely evergreen shrub, which bears dark red, bell-shaped flowers in late spring, followed by black berries, is an ideal host for clematis at any time of the year. For early spring *C. forsteri*, with its pretty green-white flowers and evergreen leaves, makes an excellent companion. Both *Pittosporum* and clematis enjoy fertile, moist but well-drained soil and full sun.

A vigorous grower like *C. forsteri* will need space, but when grown over a shrub, such as

Pittosporum 'Sandersii' hosts large, early hybrid *C.* 'Proteus' which blooms in late spring

C. forsteri, after growing through *Pittosporum*, continues through *Pinus mugo* 'Mops'

The evergreen clematis 'Early Sensation' is one of the more recent introductions. When it has finished flowering, the lovely foliage will grace this simple wire-netting fence

Pittosporum, it can also be allowed to tumble through other structural plants such as dwarf and small-growing conifers.

Clematis breeders fully appreciate the advantages of the evergreen group and one may wonder why people are not busy breeding stronger, more frost-tolerant strains. The answer is simply that they are very difficult to propagate, especially those that belong to the *armandii* group.

MID-SPRING

Macropetala and *alpina*

If your garden is too cold for evergreen clematis and a large conservatory is not at your disposal, you may have to wait until April for your first clematis show. *C. macropetala* and *C. alpina* with their beautiful purple, lilac or pink, bell-shaped flowers are well worth waiting for. Both groups are easy to care for and resistant to pests and diseases. They are hardy too and will withstand even the direst spring weather, looking lovely as they scramble through host plants.

There are many garden plants that provide virtual year-round interest. The small selection shown here may encourage you to use one or two of your feature shrubs and trees as companions to the dainty little bells of these early-flowering clematis.

Shrub hosts

Berberis thunbergii atropurpurea is a medium-sized, dense, rounded shrub with arching branches, bearing small, pale yellow flowers in mid-spring. The reddish-purple foliage is its main attraction, especially when it turns bright red in the autumn. This hardy shrub will tolerate almost any soil conditions and partial shade. Established plants need about one-quarter of their shoots cut to the base annually after flowering to promote new

growth. Wear gloves, because the thorns on the stems can be quite sharp. A deep purple *alpina* such as 'Frances Rivis' will look stunning amongst the purple-red leaves.

Evergreen shrubs play an important role in the seasonal structure of the garden and there is one that may be considered to be more beneficial to the clematis grower than any other, and that is *Camellia*. Its beautiful flowers are on show in winter and early spring when so little colour is available, and its glossy leaves provide the perfect foil for a wide range of clematis throughout the year.

Camellia prefers acid soil and to be planted away from the early morning sun, which can scorch its buds and flowers. Feed it with a balanced liquid fertilizer in mid-spring and again, if necessary, in early autumn. Apply a deep mulching of acid leaf-mould or shredded bark. Given these good conditions, *Camellia* are hardy shrubs; they grow 1–9m (3¼–29½ft) tall, depending upon the variety. Remember that clematis will require a more intensive feeding programme than the *Camellia* if these

Clematis of the *alpina* type make good companions for camellias. Here they are seen in flower together; later the seed heads will become a feature

The blooms of a pale pink *macropetala* will soon open and have the glossy leaves of *Camellia* 'E. G. Waterhouse' as their setting

95

After *Camellia* has flowered, the glossy leaves provide a perfect setting for early hybrid 'Lasurstern' in late spring.

two plants are grown together. A feeding tube inserted close to the clematis roots will make this easier to perform.

Choisya ternata (the Mexican orange blossom) is a valuable shrub for year-round interest. The sweet-scented, white flowers are borne in late spring and again in late summer and autumn. The aromatic evergreen leaves make a perfect foil for *C. alpina* or *C. macropetala*. Take your pick from those that are available to create a striking partnership. Grow *Choisya* in fertile, well-drained soil, preferably in full sun.

Euonymus fortunei 'Silver Queen' is another hardy, medium-sized shrub, growing to 2.5m (8ft). It is attractive all year round with its white-margined, evergreen leaves, the margins of which tint pink later. The greenish-white flowers, borne in spring, are rather insignificant and lend themselves to a partnership with the far superior flower of a pink *alpina* or *macropetala*. To enhance the variegation, 'Silver Queen' should be grown in full sun. Plant the clematis on the shady side to protect its roots; the flowers will soon find their way to the sun. 'Silver Queen' can also be grown as a wall shrub where she will climb to 6m (19½ft). Both the shrub and the clematis will live happily without pruning apart from what is required to keep them tidy and within limits. If the clematis becomes too entangled you can cut it back, quite low down, and let it start again with new young stems. However, don't be too enthusiastic with the secateurs if the clematis is mature with very woody stems because the shock may be too much for it; it is better to tackle the job over a couple of seasons.

Euonymus fortunei 'Silver Queen' has attractive variegated leaves all year round

'Pink Flamingo' is a beautiful *alpina* to grow with *Euonymus fortunei* 'Silver Queen'

Conifer companions

It is hard to beat a golden conifer for winter and spring interest. The size of your garden will determine the choice. *Cupressus macrocapa* 'Goldcrest' is a lovely conical shape and grows quickly to 5m (16½ft). It is good for a smaller garden and the foliage is a rich golden-yellow. *Cedrus deodara* 'Aurea' grows to a similar height but is slow growing with graceful, golden-yellow, pendant branches. *Chamaecyparis obtusa* 'Tetragona Aurea' is more bronze than yellow, especially when

grown in full sun, but with an eventual spread of 10m (33ft) it is really only suitable for a large garden. The golden leaves of conifers make a superb background for *alpina* and *macropetala* clematis.

C. alpina 'Pink Flamingo' offset by the golden-green leaves of an evergreen

A superb golden conifer provides a glowing backcloth for *C. alpina* 'Ruby'

Other supports

Macropetala and *alpina* are also ideal for growing on a fence, pergola or tripod, because although they produce a mass of flowers they are not as rampant as the late spring *montana* family. As the sepals die and fall, lovely seed heads remain to adorn the attractive foliage for many weeks. Towards the end of summer some varieties will produce a light, second flush of flowers.

A tripod set into a border, planted with *macropetala* or *alpina*, together with a mid-season hybrid will bring many months of colour. The dainty bells of the early variety will be a picture in April and May and the attractive leaves and seed heads will provide a pleasant setting for the large flowers of the hybrid during the summer when it may be joined by a few heads of the early bells having their second flush.

Tripods are an ideal way to bring height to the garden. Small shrubs or perennials planted

C. 'Lady Northcliffe', a mid-season hybrid that is ideal for growing on a tripod, with a pink *macropetala* as its companion

around the base will help to shade the clematis roots and there is the opportunity to create some very pleasing combinations. You can take your pick of the *macropetala* or *alpina* varieties because they are all quite compact in

C. alpina 'Frances Rivis' is a good choice for a pergola

size. Mid-season hybrids can be quite rampant growers, so choose one of the smaller varieties. Here are a few suggested pairings:

❦ *C. alpina* 'Frankie' (mid-blue) planted with C. 'Gillian Blades' (white with golden stamens). Shade the roots with a small evergreen shrub such as *Daphne laureola* (1m (3¼ft) high, 1.5m (5ft) spread). The glossy evergreen leaves provide year-round interest and the clusters of slightly fragrant yellow-green flowers in early spring are followed by black fruits.

❦ *C. macropetala* 'Markhams Pink' planted with C. 'Lady Northcliffe' (deep blue). A group of *Erica carnea* 'Springwood Pink' would be a good choice for base planting. The pretty pale pink flowers bloom in early spring and deepen with age. Being evergreen, this small, trailing shrub will provide year-round interest and shade for the clematis roots. This variety of heather will withstand mildly alkaline soil.

Both of the above combinations can be planted in sun or partial shade.

❦ *C. macropetala* (the original lavender-blue species) with C. 'Guernsey Cream' is a combination best planted in a shady border to protect 'Guernsey Cream's' delicate colour. An ideal base plant is *Asarum europaeum*, an evergreen creeping perennial with kidney-shaped, glossy, dark green leaves, which also enjoys a shady location. The purple flowers in spring are of little significance as the attractive leaves mostly hide them. This plant thrives in humus-rich, moist, but well-drained soil, preferably acid or neutral.

❦ *Macropetala* and *alpina* types are ideal for growing in a container. Once they have flowered their pretty leaves can provide background height for surrounding pots filled with colourful flowers.

A long-flowering, mid-season hybrid, such as 'Ernest Markham', makes an ideal companion for *C. macropetala* or *C. alpina*

The advantage of growing *macropetala* and *alpina* through other climbers is that it enables them to reach a height which allows us to look up into their bells and admire the beauty of their stamens and anthers. The twisted,

C. 'Guernsey Cream' should be planted in the shade to protect its delicate colour

C. macropetala seed heads complement a young *Wisteria* growing on a house wall

C. 'Frances Rivis' seed heads frame *Rosa* 'New Dawn'

hardwood stems of *Wisteria* make an ideal support; clematis usually flowers a little earlier, but the partnership of clematis flowers and wisteria racemes as they form is most attractive and the clematis seed heads look lovely when the wisteria is in full bloom. The clematis will not grow to more than about 3m (10ft), so it will only ramble along the lower branches of the wisteria. There is more about wisteria in Chapter 4: Summer Splendour.

A climbing rose can be used to support *macropetala* or *alpina*; the clematis flowers will add interest before the rose blooms and their silvery seed heads will be an added attraction later, a glistening framework to enhance the rose's beauty.

These charming early clematis are so easy to care for and such a delight to see that they really are a must for even the smallest garden.

LATE SPRING

Montana

The massed blooms of *Clematis montana* in May will cheer even the greyest day and when viewed against a bright blue sky they really are magnificent. *Montana* is a vigorous species and needs a lot of space. When grown through a tree it can spread to its heart's content and the sky becomes its backdrop.

The rampant growth of *montana* will swamp all but the largest of shrubs; it is preferable therefore to grow them alone on walls or fences at the back of a border or on house walls.

▲ *C. montana* 'Pictons' beautifully supported by a conifer's sweeping branches

▼ The blue skies of May provide the perfect backdrop for *C. montana* as it clambers through a tree

C. montana blooms to great effect on a pergola

▲ Large coniferous trees make ideal companions for
C. montana

▼ *C. montana* 'Marjorie' tumbles through the branches
of *Prunus* 'Pink Perfection'

If you are seeking to create a shady arbour under a pergola, take your choice from the beautiful range of *montana* varieties. In May and June sweetly scented flowers will surround you and for the remainder of the summer and into early autumn the attractive leaves will continue to provide a dense, lush covering.

▲ Pink *C. montana* adorns the walls of this picturesque cottage in May

▶ *C. montana* climbing over a doorway

▼ White *C. montana* clothing a large wall

Clematis breeders continue to produce stunning new hybrids, such as this one named 'Caroline'

'Nelly Moser' has a second, lighter flush later in the summer. Here she is seen growing with 'Ville de Lyon'

Early, large-flowered cultivars

Clematis breeders have done a wonderful job in producing such an incredible range of early, large-flowered varieties. They flower during May and June, then take a break to recover their strength to flower again in September.

The bright pink 'Nelly Moser' with her distinctive stripe is probably one of the most well known of this group and she is seen in May gracing many a garden fence or porch. Nelly, like many of this group, is quite hardy and unless nipped by frost will produce an abundance of large, showy blooms through May and into June.

Not all of the early hybrids are quite as hardy; a lot depends upon their parentage. With so much breeding having taken place since the first recorded cross fertilization between *C. integrifolia* and *C. viticella* by Mr. Henderson in 1835 – which produced *C. x eriostemon* 'Hendersonii' – parentage has now become quite a complex issue. When you buy one of these hybrids from a reputable nursery they will advise you of its susceptibility to wilt and the general sturdiness of the variety. It is not easy to generalize, however. One garden may be able to grow a beauty such as 'Vyvyan Pennel' without a moment's setback, while in another it may die away and recover two or three times before it finally settles.

With so many clematis to choose from within this group and with such a variety of ways for them to be partnered with other plants, you can create a unique late-spring garden that will be colourful through to the summer.

Choosing colours

The colour range is vast, so including clematis in a colour-coordinated scheme will be relatively easy. You may have to use other genus for true yellow in the border – the closest the early-flowering clematis can get to it is 'Wada's Primrose' – and a really true blue

'Miss Bateman' was introduced in 1869. She is now one of the older members of this group

C. x eriostemon 'Hendersonii', the earliest recorded cross-fertilized hybrid

is hard to find, although 'Multi Blue' with its silver reverse has only the slightest tinge of purple. A spring border devoted to two or three colours can look very effective and it is currently fashionable to coordinate pots and features into a tonal colour scheme. Fortunately, gardening does not have to follow fashion. More importantly, it is a wonderful way to express your own personality. Nature allows a riot of colours such as purple, magenta and red, to live happily together and if this projects your personality, then go for it. The large-flowered clematis of spring and summer will help you to be creative.

Having already promoted 'Nelly Moser' as a bright, cheerful early hybrid to grow along the fence or around the porch, there are of course many other ways that this popular

Soft and gentle *C.* 'Guernsey Cream'

Bright and vibrant *C.* 'Prince Philip'

A PLANTING PLAN FOR GREEN AND WHITE
(WITH A HINT OF YELLOW)

The trellis at the back of this bed could screen unwanted visual intrusions such as a dustbin, washing line or storage tank. Although the planting emphasis here is a fresh, light, spring display, the *Phormium* and *Osmanthus* provide structure for most of the year. If the spring bulbs are interspersed with summer flowering bulbs such as white lilies, the rose and clematis will ensure that the green and white theme continues all summer long.

When preparing this border for planting, dig in plenty of humus-rich compost, because many of the plants selected for this planting plan require fertile, free-draining soil in order to flourish.

1 *Clematis* 'Arctic Queen'. Large, fully double, white flowers, the outer sepals often tinged green. Blooms in May, June and September. Grows to 2.5–3m (8–10ft). The creamy stamens complement the rose

2 *Clematis flammula*. Small, white, star-shaped flowers with almond scent. Blooms July–October. Grows to 4m (13ft)

3 Climbing rose 'Rive D'or'

4 *Phormium cookianum* 'Cream Delight'. Broad, arching, creamy-yellow leaves with narrow bands along the margins. Tubular,

A PLANTING PLAN FOR GREEN AND WHITE (WITH A HINT OF YELLOW)

▲ 'Arctic Queen' flowers in May, June and September

▲ Climbing rose 'Rive D'or' complements the creamy stamens of 'Arctic Queen'

▶ *Phormium cookianum* provides year-round interest

yellow-green flowers, in upright panicles in summer. Height: 2m (6½ft). Spread: 3m (10ft)

5 *Camassia leichtlinii.* Long spires bearing star-shaped, white flowers in summer. Soil must be kept moist. Height: 1.3m (4½ft). Spread: 10cm (4in)

6 *Osmanthus heterophyllus* 'Gulftide'. Dense, rounded shrub with holly-like leaves. Small, white, tubular flowers appear from the summer to the autumn, followed by very dark blue fruit. Although it can grow to 2.5m (8ft), it will tolerate hard pruning to keep its shape and size within the symmetry of this border design

7 *Anemone blanda* 'White Splendour'. Clump-forming, tuberous perennial with large white flowers in spring

8 *Erythronium californicum* 'White Beauty'. Bulbous perennial. Creamy-white flowers with recurved tepals, born on graceful stems. Prefers dappled shade and must be kept moist

9 *Galanthus* (snowdrops) will bring a touch of brightness in winter/early spring

10 *Crocus.* Any white variety. To follow the snowdrops

11 *Narcissus.* Any white or pale yellow varieties or a mixture of both

'Nelly Moser' brings a splash of colour to a hydrangea before the shrub's own flowers appear

The golden stamens of 'Gillian Blades' highlight the small flowers of *Corokia* 'Coppershine'

hybrid can be grown. If you can avoid continuous direct sunlight so much the better, for this will fade her bright pink sepals. When growing 'Nelly Moser' or any other clematis through a shrub, there are choices to be made. If the shrub is of a flowering variety, do you want to enjoy those flowers on their own or would they be enhanced by a clematis as a flowering companion? Much will depend upon the nature of the shrub's flowers. Azaleas, for instance, are often so dense and vivid that the addition of another flower would be quite overwhelming. On the other hand, some shrubs have small, quite insignificant flowers which clematis could help to highlight.

If you have decided that the clematis and shrub should not bloom together, then you need to consider who blooms first. For example, 'Nelly Moser' will bloom before a hydrangea but after a magnolia. Both shrubs make ideal hosts for this clematis and are enhanced by Nelly's presence.

Magnolia provides a magnificent spring display

Good companions

Hydrangea is a popular genus with 80 or more species, but it is the mop head and lace cap *macrophylla* varieties that are most commonly seen in gardens. *Paniculata*, with its white, cone-shaped flowers is becoming more widespread; so too is the climbing species *petorialis*, a vigorous climber bearing a mass of white flowers during summer, perfect for clothing a north-facing wall. Clematis can be successfully grown through most hydrangeas although it may become a little buried in the verdant *petorialis* climber. Clematis will also enjoy the conditions that are best for hydrangeas: humus-rich, well-drained, fertile soil and protection from strong winds. If the pH balance of the soil is below 5.5, these acid conditions will produce blue hydrangea flowers; above this pH and the alkalinity will create pink flowers.

Magnolias need similar conditions to *Camellia*. Unlike the latter, however, some varieties will tolerate alkaline soil. *M. x soulangeana* prefers acid or neutral conditions and has a number of offspring with flowers ranging from white to pink to deep purple depending upon type. As beautiful as they are, they can only really be accommodated in a large garden as they can reach 7m (23ft) with a very wide spread.

M. stellata is a compact variety for the smaller garden and will grow in alkaline soil. Magnolia blossoms are so spectacular that it is a shame to detract from them; their attractive leaves, however, provide a perfect setting for a clematis that blooms a little later.

Experimenting with plant and clematis combinations is a very rewarding challenge

The magnolia blooms have finished, leaving the stage empty for 'Nelly Moser'

and with an abundance of early, large-flowered clematis available and an almost endless list of attractive shrubs and climbers, late spring offers a myriad choices. Here are just a few ideas using some old favourites and a few of the more unusual hosts.

The fruit of *Actinidia kolomikta*, a relative of *A. deliciosa*, the kiwi fruit plant, is not of edible quality, but as a garden climber it is far superior. The heart-shaped deciduous leaves are tinted purple when young and turn dark green with white and pink tips as they develop. The small, white flowers in June are rather insignificant. When grown to its full potential on a warm, sunny wall, in well-drained, fertile soil, *A. kolomikta* can reach 5m (16½ft) or more, making an impressive sight with its

'Asao' flowers in May and makes a perfect partner for *Actinidia kolomikta*

This purple hybrid has the choice of clambering up the tree or through the magnolia. Eventually it may do both

Actinidia kolomikta, a spectacular wall shrub with unusual-coloured leaves in spring

green, pink and white leaves. The lovely deep pink clematis 'Asao', which blooms in May, will enhance the overall effect. Neither require much pruning, just enough to keep them looking beautiful. 'Asao' forms unusual seed heads which can be used effectively in flower arrangements.

Ceanothus is another shrub that enjoys the support and protection of a wall where it can make twice the height of those planted in an open and exposed site. The Californian lilac requires full sun to develop its mass of blue flowers which are borne in spring, summer or autumn, depending upon the variety. Although it is lime tolerant, the leaves will occasionally turn yellow with chlorosis and require a treatment of sequestered iron. An annual acid

C. 'Margaret Hunt' has been trained against a high wall to mingle with *Ceanothus* 'Autumnal Blue'. The delicate pink may fade in direct sunlight

mulch may also help to alleviate this problem. Like many shrubs, *Ceanothus* enjoys fertile, well-drained, friable soil. Pink clematis provides a lovely contrast to the blue *Ceanothus*, but most of the pale pink varieties fade in full sunlight. The stronger rose-pink of 'Dr. Ruppel', with its paler margins and cerise stripes, is more able to withstand the sun's bleaching effect. This is another combination that needs little pruning.

When we think of *Salvia*, the bright scarlet variety *splendens,* which we grow as an annual, usually comes to mind. However, this enormous genus of plants includes some charming and unusual shrub-type plants. *S. microphylla-grahamii,* for example, has attractive evergreen leaves and magenta-pink flowers over a long period. It does not grow very tall, only 1m (3¼ft), making it an ideal specimen shrub for the middle of a border. Although it can be cut back in severe weather, it is certainly not as tender as *splendens,* especially if it is protected from cold winds. *Clematis* 'Snow Queen' with her large, white, wavy-edged flowers makes a good companion for this pretty shrub.

Cestrum 'Newellii' is larger; its vigorous, evergreen branches can grow to 3m (10ft).

Bring something different to the shrub border by growing *Salvia microphylla* with *Clematis* 'Snow Queen'

Cestrum 'Newellii' and *Clematis* 'Corona', two vibrant colours together

The tubular, crimson flowers are followed by purple-red berries. For a vibrant partnership, pair it with *Clematis* 'Corona'. They can be planted in full sun or partial shade in rich, friable, free-draining soil. 'Newellii' will benefit from the protection of a wall, although it can be grown free-standing in a sheltered bed. Both plants will need only minimal pruning.

Robinia pseudoacacia 'Frisia' is a tree that is frequently seen in gardens, popular because of its beautiful golden-yellow foliage. Sadly its shrub relative, *Robinia hispida*, is rarely seen, although its leaves are equally as lovely and the deep rose-pink racemes that bloom from late spring through to summer really are a spectacle. It is quite a trouble-free plant and fully hardy, not too fussy about soil, although it prefers moist, well-drained conditions. Like clematis, it does not tolerate too much wind, but on the whole it is an easy shrub and it is

Robinia hispida and an early hybrid clematis make a wonderful late-spring partnership

a mystery why it is not more popular. Maybe it is because of its size; with a height and spread of 3m (10ft), perhaps it is a little big for the average garden. If you have the space, just imagine that huge shrub covered in large racemes of pink flowers surrounded by the beautiful leaves. Add a hybrid clematis of your choice and you will create quite a picture.

Early-flowering clematis hybrids need little pruning, which makes them ideal partners for a small tree. Choose one of the taller-growing varieties if you want it to climb through the branches. Just two good choices would be *Clematis* 'Belle Nantaise', whose large, pale

◄ A pear tree makes a productive host for 'Nelly Moser'. You can enjoy the clematis in spring and the fruit later

▼ A few twigs have been inserted into the ground to give *C.* Josephine ('Evijohill') some support as she makes effective and beautiful ground cover

lavender-blue flowers will bloom from June to September, and rich red 'Ernest Markham', which can still be seen flowering into October.

Because of their need for water and nourishment, clematis should not be planted directly into the lawn. Plant it into a nearby bed and train it up into the tree, or make a circle bed around the tree that it can be kept well nourished by the timely application of fertilizers and mulch.

Unlike the earlier, small clematis, whose stamens are only on view if we are able to look up under their bell-shaped sepals, the lovely centres of the large, saucer-shaped flowers of the hybrids are best seen straight on or from above. Clematis make very effective ground cover plants, but growing them in this way provides easy dining for slugs, snails and other pests, so you may have to take extra precautions. A group of low-growing, evergreen shrubs such as *Hebe* 'Karl Teschner' lifts the clematis away from the ground. Alternatively, small twigs pushed into the soil will provide support.

Whatever you choose as their companions, a selection of early hybrid clematis will ensure that your garden is full of glorious colour as spring makes way for summer.

4

SUMMER
SPLENDOUR

What can be more splendid than a beautiful garden on a bright sunny day in June? The freshness of spring still lingers whilst the temperate weather encourages a multitude of flowers to burst into bloom – roses, perennials, summer bedding plants, lilies, seasonal-flowering shrubs.

Clematis will be growing at an alarming rate, so continue to check those on fences, walls and pergolas to ensure they have plenty of places to wind their tendrils. Those growing over shrubs and trees usually find enough natural support, but occasionally, when they outgrow their companion or the wind blows them off course, they will clamber up an

A late, large-flowered 'Ville de Lyon' provides a bright, bold backcloth to the lime-green of a young *Choisya* shrub; the blue hydrangea provides contrast and the colours are drawn together by a bright pink dahlia

entirely new host and you are left with the delicate task of redirecting them.

As summer progresses, the demand for water usually increases and reservoirs face the challenge of coping with national demand. Rationing is often inevitable and the thick mulching you applied earlier in the year will help to retain moisture and keep the root run cool. A tube inserted at the time of planting will ensure that the content of the watering can reaches the roots, which is where it is most needed. June and July are the peak months for clematis and it is a superb time to visit gardens where they are featured to gain inspiration and ideas for companion planting.

The early-season, large-flowered clematis that commenced blooming in May are still bountiful in June, quickly followed by the late, large-flowered varieties. These are the showpieces of summer with their big, bold blooms demanding attention as they tumble

C. viticella 'Margot Koster' clothes an old stone wall with an abundance of blooms

The herbaceous *C. jouiniana* 'Praecox' and *Lathyrus grandiflorus* (everlasting sweet pea) make a rampant partnership as they tumble through the border together

C. viticella 'Venosa Violacea' and *Abutilon*, with a collection of graceful pots and urns, create a pleasant display to be enjoyed on the patio

through shrubs and roses, climb walls, archways and pergolas or make a beautiful backcloth to the colourful summer border.

Although a little less flamboyant than their large-flowered relatives, many clematis enthusiasts consider the *viticella* forms to be even more beautiful. They are vigorous and hardy, so whether you choose a variety with dainty bells or saucer-shaped flowers, you will enjoy an abundance of blooms from mid-summer to mid-autumn.

Clematis of the herbaceous group are not seen nearly as frequently in gardens as those of the climbing species. It is a pity, because they make lovely partners for roses, shrubs and summer flowers as they weave their way through the summer border.

Clematis planted in large containers make a wonderful display on the patio, but they are only for the gardener dedicated to a consistent watering and feeding programme. If you have the time and inclination to water the containers twice daily during dry spells, some exciting combinations can be produced: vibrant colours to excite and stimulate or soft tones to sooth and relax. It is also an opportunity to grow one of the more tender varieties in a container, as long as you are able to move the heavy soil-filled container into a frost-free environment during the winter.

During the latter part of the season texensis, *orientalis* and late species clematis join the summer collection. As a feature of the autumn scene they are included in the next chapter.

SUMMER COMPANIONS

As you stroll through a summer garden enjoying the heady scent of roses, the beauty of the flower border or a flowering shrub, pause here and there to consider how clematis could enhance the existing scene. There may be bare patches to fill, new borders to make, or a whole new garden to create if the house is new or if the garden has been neglected. Planting clematis in partnership with roses, shrubs and flowers can ensure a summer full of colour and interest.

Clematis with roses

Clematis and roses make excellent partners, as their cultural needs are similar: they both enjoy well-drained, fertile soil, good food and plenty to drink. Meet these needs and apply mulching each spring and they will live happily together, giving an abundance of colour for many years.

We have the choice of planting clematis to flower before, with, or after the rose. In practice, there nearly always seems to be a period when they are in flower at the same time so it is important to choose compatible colours.

As already mentioned, a climbing rose can be used to great effect to support clematis before the rose blooms and there is a large selection of early-flowering varieties that

C. 'Rhapsody', a recent hybrid introduction, bears beautiful indigo-blue flowers from June to September, which are shown to perfection with the salmon-pink flowers of bush rose 'Silver Jubilee'

C. 'Arctic Queen', C. 'The President' and *Rosa* 'Handel' on an old stone wall

C. 'Vyvyan Pennell' often bears double flowers in May, although this young bloom is not sure what it is. It blooms before the rose and again in September

The rose is in bud and will soon join mid-season hybrid C. 'William Kennet'. Together they will provide a lovely display throughout the summer

bloom in May and early June that would fulfil this purpose admirably.

When we want the rose and clematis to flower together, we turn to what are known as the mid-season, large-flowered varieties. They flower from June to September.

To enjoy the rose on its own and the clematis later, we can choose the clematis from the late, large-flowering cultivars – the *viticella*, *texensis* and *orientalis* forms – and the late species.

Repeat- or continuous-flowering roses usually have a period when blooms are sparse,

C. 'Huldine' blooms continuously from June to September. Here it is partnered with rose 'Raymond Chenault'

▲ *C.* 'Caroline', another recent introduction to the early hybrids, makes a lovely partner for Bourbon rose 'Mme. Isaac Pereire'

▶ The curled sepals of late-flowering 'Madame Grangé' bring colour and interest as the rose blooms become sparse

▼ Climbing rose 'New Dawn' and mid-season hybrid *C.* 'Sealand Gem' bloom happily together all summer

C. viticella 'Alba Luxurians' flowers from July to September. It is seen here with the splendid bush rose 'Josephine Bruce'

between the initial flush and their second display. Clematis selected to harmonize or contrast will ensure a colourful array all summer long.

On climbing roses, train clematis both horizontally and vertically to encourage an even distribution of blooms. One climbing rose could play host to two clematis. An early, large-flowered hybrid will add colour before the rose comes into bloom and can be followed by a late-season variety. There may be a period when all three are flowering together – in a softly harmonious combination or a vibrant display of contrasts.

As the season progresses, the lower leaves of some clematis varieties become brown. By planting clematis behind the rose, unsightly leaves can be hidden and the rose will provide shade for the clematis roots. Shrub roses and rambling roses are ideal for this purpose.

Late-flowering *C.* 'Jackmanii' and 'Ville de Lyon' with climbing rose 'Handel' create a vibrant trio on a house wall

Herbaceous C. 'Durandii' will continue to flower long after rambling rose 'Dorothy Perkins' has finished

Climbing clematis have a tendency to overpower smaller roses such as hybrid tea and bush roses, so choose instead from the non-twining herbaceous group of clematis (listed on pages 52–55), allowing them to meander informally through the border and wend their way through the roses.

The border plan shown on pages 124–5 demonstrates how three 'Chinatown' bush roses can be grown with early and late clematis and other plants – cistus, roscoea, elymus, campanula and gentiana – to provide a long season of harmonizing yellow and blue. A high wall, fence or trellis at the back of the border is required to support the climbing plants and create the 'backdrop'.

Many of the old shrub and rambling roses, such as 'Françoise Juranville' give a magnificent display in summer, but unlike modern roses they rarely repeat flowering.

Rambling rose 'Françoise Juranville' and C. viticella 'Purpurea Plena Elegans' blooming in perfect harmony. This is an old-fashioned partnership that works particularly well in any garden

YELLOW AND BLUE PLANTING PLAN

▲ Clematis hybrid 'Perle d'Azur'

◄ Climbing rose 'Maigold'

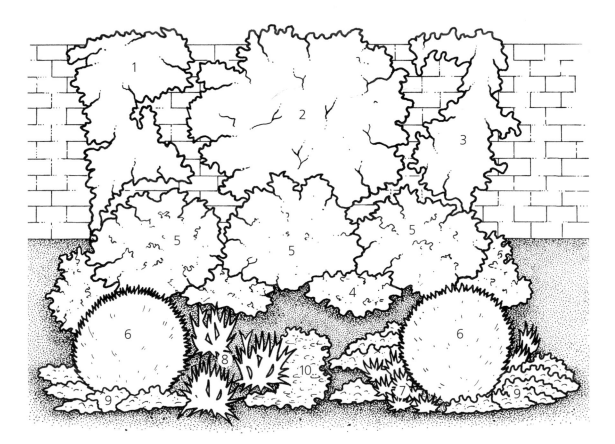

YELLOW AND BLUE

Blue shades of clematis and yellow roses feature in this bright summer border. For a long flowering season, the location should be south or west facing. Under-plant with yellow and blue spring bulbs for a spring display.

1 *Clematis macropetala*. Violet-blue, bell-shaped flowers. Early summer

2 Climbing rose 'Maigold'. Bronze-yellow. Fragrant. Summer

3 *Clematis* 'Perle d'Azur'. Azure-blue, open, bell-shaped flowers. Summer to autumn

4 *Clematis* 'Durandii'. Herbaceous. Non-twining. Deep indigo-blue with yellow anthers

5 Bush rose 'Chinatown'. Double, yellow, scented blooms. Summer to autumn

6 *Cistus x corbarienses*. Evergreen, busy, dense shrub. Masses of white flowers with central yellow blotches. Late spring and early summer.

7 *Roscoea cauteloides* 'Kew Beauty'. Pale yellow, orchid-like flowers; early summer

8 *Elymus magellanicus* (rye grass). Densely tufted; intense blue; mound forming

9 *Campanula* 'Chewtown Joy'. Carpet forming; purple-blue bells; all summer

10 *Gentiana* 'Sino-ornata'. Semi-evergreen; deep blue, trumpet-shaped flowers; late summer to autumn

Clematis 'Durandii' and bush rose 'Canary Bird', a vibrant combination for summer

Clematis of the *viticella* group have a rather 'old fashioned' appeal of their own and make good companions to these old roses. *Viticella* clematis begin to bloom in July, just as the rose starts to fade; they may share a short time together, so choose complementary colours.

When the rose has finished, the clematis will continue to flower for a few more weeks.

Climbers and wall shrubs

By creating colour at eye level and above with climbers, a new dimension is introduced.

C. 'Rouge Cardinal' makes a dramatic backdrop with fellow climber, wisteria

Summer offers the greatest choice for climbers. Unfortunately, some of the best are frost tender and need to be treated as annuals in most parts of Britain and Northern Europe. *Cobaea scandens*, the delightful cup-and-saucer plant, is a typical example, along with *Thunbergia alata* (black-eyed Susan) and *Tropaeolum peregrinum* (Canary creeper). Plants can be brought along from seed in a greenhouse and planted out alongside a clematis, when all danger of frost has past, to create an impressive summer show.

Clianthus puniceus, a climber originating from New Zealand, has long, fern-like, dark green leaves, which offset the brilliant red flowers, reminiscent of lobsters' claws. *C. albus*, the white version, is often flushed green. This plant may survive the winter in

C. viticella 'Purpurea Plena Elegans' and *Tropaeolum peregrinum* (Canary creeper) make bright summer companions. The Canary creeper, an annual climber, is not frost hardy

Clianthus puniceus has exotic red flowers in spring

The leaves of *Clianthus* provide a perfect frame for *viticella* 'Margot Koster' from July to September

The beautiful passion flower can make a good companion for clematis, especially on a large pergola

mild climate zones if planted against a warm, south-facing wall and protected by fleece during prolonged frost.

There are a few varieties of *Passiflora* (passion flower) that will withstand a moderate amount of frost if planted in a warm, sheltered site and if the wood has ripened well throughout the summer. Being evergreen and rampant, they can provide a green covering on a large pergola throughout the winter, or they can be used to clothe a wall or fence. When nipped by frost, the leaves tend to have a rather droopy appearance, but during the summer their beautiful and unusual flowers are quite spectacular.

Chaenomeles japonica (Japanese quince or simply 'Japonica') is fully hardy; it is not a climber, but an evergreen shrub that enjoys the support of a wall. Between the long, spring flowering season and the autumn fruits that can be used to make delicious jam, the shrub

127

Chaenomeles japonica (Japanese quince) is easily trained around a window

C. 'Hagley Hybrid' creates a stunning summer display, but will fade if grown in full sun

can serve as a willing host to a summer-flowering clematis such as 'Hagley Hybrid'. Quince is particularly useful for growing on a house wall because it lends itself to being trained under and around windows. It does not object to partial shade, which is ideal for this partnership because the delicate pink 'Hagley Hybrid' will fade if grown in full sun.

Some of the genus of evergreen *Pyracantha* can play a similar role to that of the quince, because their framework of branches can also be trained around windows and doorways. They can be grown as a border shrub or against a fence. Whatever site you choose, they provide a lovely framework for clematis to climb. Bright orange or red berries follow the clusters of creamy white flowers born in June.

One of the most breathtaking sights of early summer is that of *Wisteria* in full bloom. The long racemes of purple, lavender or white need no distracting companions. Walking under a wisteria-clad pergola is one of the best ways to appreciate their beauty. You can plant clematis and roses as companions to flower after the wisteria for a long and colourful season. Bear in mind that a very solid structure will be needed to support so many strong-growing climbers together. An established wisteria requires pruning twice a year. In late summer remove all the unwanted growth and prune the remaining stems to 15cm (6in) of the main branch. Mid-winter is the time to reduce the stems to 10cm (4in) leaving only two or three buds.

Often, the only space available that is large enough to support a full-grown wisteria is a house wall, for it is not unusual for these

▶ The lingering remains of a wisteria are almost obscured by a collection of clematis and roses on the upright of this pergola. White rambling rose 'Seagull' and climbing rose 'Summer Wine' harmonize with *Clematis* 'Rouge Cardinal'

▼ *C.* 'Jackmanii Alba' has been beautifully framed by *Pyracantha* flowers

C. 'Jackmanii Rubra' and wisteria make good companions for a pergola

plants to reach 9m (29½ft) or more. When the flowers begin to fade, the graceful branches and elegantly formed leaves will provide a delightful setting for clematis such as 'Jackmanii Rubra', which will flower for a long period.

There are approximately 180 species of *Lonicera*, but not all of them are hardy or emit the wonderful perfume we associate with common honeysuckle, or woodbine. Few things conjure up summer more effectively in our minds than a comfortable garden seat, a glass of cold lemonade, warm sun, blue skies, birds singing, bees buzzing and the scent of honeysuckle filling the air. If you want to provide a haven like this in your garden, remember to site your seat to the east of the honeysuckle so that its delightful perfume wafts over you on the prevailing westerly summer breezes.

A magnificent sight in early summer, wisteria covers the front of this old stone cottage

Lonicera is a rampant grower and comes in evergreen, semi-evergreen and deciduous varieties, the latter usually having the strongest perfume. It can look equally as good climbing walls, fences and pergolas, and being of a similar climbing habit to clematis it clambers just as effectively over shrubs and up into trees. However its growth is denser and it can dominate smaller shrubs.

Honeysuckle and clematis climbing together can make an impressive display and once again clematis can extend the honeysuckle's season. A word of caution, however: if you place two strong-growing characters together, they may fight for dominance, so choose less-rampant varieties from both genera, and ensure they have a good deep root run and are well watered and fed. *Lonicera x americana* has strongly fragrant, creamy-yellow flowers flushed pink all summer long, whilst *L. periclymenum* 'Serotina' bears fragrant yellow-red flowers in the months of July and August. Both of these plants will grow to approximately 4m (13ft). Choose a

C. 'Lady Northcliff' flowers a little earlier than honeysuckle and will continue all summer long

large-flowered clematis for a bold display or, alternatively, the slightly more subtle effect of a purple or wine-red *viticella*. A pergola can provide the perfect location for honeysuckle and clematis, with the honeysuckle climbing up one support, the clematis another, and both intermingling where they meet at the top.

Clematis as a backcloth in the border

Given the right location and setting, clematis can be used either singly or in pairs to create a stunning backcloth to a border. Many front gardens have a border adjacent to the house

◄ Early large hybrid 'Vyvyan Pennell' produces single blooms for its second show, providing height and interest at the back of this brightly coloured, late-summer border

▼ Late, large hybrid 'Jackmanii', an old favourite of the author, provides a lovely backcloth to this colourful front garden border

and the house wall can be put to good effect in this way. Fences, trellises and garden walls are invaluable supports at the back of any border and they add another vital dimension.

Clematis with shrubs and trees

When all of the garden walls and fences are covered there are still plenty of opportunities to grow clematis through shrubs and trees.

Clematis that require hard pruning make ideal companions for spring-flowering shrubs such as camellia, magnolia, rhododendron and azaleas. Clematis climb their way through the shrubs during spring and early summer, but do not compete with the spring show.

▶ The large, purple flowers of 'The President' together with 'Ville de Lyon', make a bright, bold backcloth

▼ The smaller flowers of *viticella* 'Kermesina' and the velvet sheen of 'Gipsy Queen' flowers will grace the back of any border from July to September

Golden-leaved *Physocarpus* and wine-red *C. viticella* 'Kermesina' make a stunning partnership

R. 'Luteum' is one of the few rhododendrons with a perfume. Here it is planted in a half-barrel filled with ericaceous compost. Mid-season clematis 'Elsa Späth' will follow a little later

Later they come into their own and bring another season of flowering beauty.

If clematis is the 'Queen of Climbers', as she is fondly referred to, then camellia is her 'King'. You can hardly go wrong when choosing a clematis to grow against the lovely glossy leaves of a camellia. The only problem is finding situations in the garden where the blooms will not be scorched by the early morning sun.

There is an extensive range of azaleas and rhododendrons, but do not consider planting them in the border unless it is of acid soil. If your soil is neutral or alkaline, plant them instead in ericaceous compost in a container placed in a partially shaded spot on the patio, away from morning sun and cold winds. This family of shrubs requires shallow planting and regular feeding. Deadhead them after they have flowered to encourage leaf growth rather than the formation of seed. Enjoy the spring spectacle and, later, a show of your favourite summer-flowering clematis.

The medium-sized shrub physocarpus will grow 2–3m (6½–10ft) and shares clematis' love of moist, fertile, well-drained soil, preferably acid or neutral. The beautiful golden leaves provide a superb background for deep wine-red clematis.

There are many shrubs that will grow in either an acid or alkaline soil. Two flowering, deciduous shrubs belonging to this category are weigela and kolkwitzia. The difference is in their size. Weigela should be pruned after flowering and allowed to grow to a maximum of 1.5–2m (5–6½ft), whereas kolkwitzia, the beauty bush, can reach 2.5–3m (8–10ft) and pruning is not so imperative. Both of these shrubs should be given space in the border so that you can enjoy their arching branches festooned with a mass of pink, bell-shaped flowers in late spring/early summer. Later, these graceful branches can support summer-flowering clematis, maybe a *viticella* for the smaller shrub and a large-flowered variety for the beauty bush, choosing colours to complement other plants within the border.

Syringa vulgaris, the common lilac, is a large shrub or small tree that will grow in any soil but thrives in chalk. It is a great favourite with gardeners and rightly so, with its lilac, purple or white panicles of flowers wafting the sweetest of scents. It is sad when their

Weigela 'Looymansii Aurea', a lovely shrub to host a clematis

The mauve-pink flowers of late hybrid 'Margaret Hunt' perfectly complement this lace-cap hydrangea

Large-flowered hybrid 'Victoria' extends the season for this lilac shrub

short season in late spring and early summer comes to an end so quickly. Whilst clematis falls short on perfume, their magnificent flowers can bring life to an otherwise rather colourless shrub right through summer into early autumn.

In spring, hydrangea was shown supporting 'Nelly Moser' before the shrub's own flowers had formed. Hydrangeas and clematis look lovely when they flower together, especially if the hydrangea is one of the lace-cap varieties.

The strident yellow flowers of hypericum make it a difficult shrub to place in a border, but if you have a dull corner or want a bold focus, this is the shrub to choose. There are a large number of different varieties, ranging from dwarf species to large shrubs and they are mostly very easy to grow. A deep purple clematis makes a good contrast to the bright yellow flowers.

The pink flowers of late hybrid 'Comtesse de Bouchard' is an unusual choice as a companion for the *Hypericum* 'Jack Elliot', but demonstrates how experimenting with colour combinations can produce superb results

Cotoneaster, a family of deciduous, semi-evergreen or evergreen shrubs and trees, is an excellent choice for any garden. They bear white or pink flowers in the spring/early summer and orange or red berries in autumn. Birds love the berries and a flock of redwings can virtually consume a whole tree or shrub on a cold winter's day. The prostrate, ground-cover varieties provide good support for small hybrids or *viticella* clematis; the larger evergreen shrubs are superb companions for any summer-flowering clematis. An early, large-flowered clematis would be a good choice for a cotoneaster tree because they both require very little pruning.

Winter and early spring are the seasons when evergreen shrubs are most valued, but they also make good hosts for clematis at any time of the year. Choose deep-coloured clematis without stripes for the variegated varieties, such as eleagnus, or the combination may look too busy.

Early hybrid 'Carnaby' finds a good home in a cotoneaster tree

Osmanthus heterophyllus 'Aureovarecata' is the perfect host for *Clematis* 'Proteus'

Bright and bold, 'Ville de Lyon' takes over as the blooms of escallonia fade

The larger shrubs of pittosporum, as described in the spring chapter, can play host to clematis all year if given a warm and protected location. Their attractive glossy leaves will enhance almost any summer clematis, and they look particularly good with a deep-purple *viticella*. Alternatively, the purple-leaved variety *P.* 'Tom Thumb' forms a low shrub 100 x 60cm (3¼ x 2ft); two or three planted together provide excellent low-level support for a clematis.

Ilex (holly), whether plain or variegated, is another fine evergreen companion. The clematis flowers are followed by bright holly berries. Choose a self-fertile variety or grow a male and a female together or the berries will not form. *Osmanthus heterophyllus* looks very similar to holly and provides an equally lovely foil for summer clematis.

Escallonia is a family of small or medium-sized shrubs, bearing glossy evergreen leaves

Clematis 'Jackmanii' gracing a variegated shrub

with pink, red or white flowers in spring or summer. Choose clematis to complement the escallonia flowers or to take over when they have finished.

C. viticella 'Etoile Violette' finds its own way into this pittosporum, growing well within the protection of a south-facing wall at Marwood Gardens, north Devon

A vibrant partnership: *Clematis* 'Edomurasaki' with *Potentilla* 'Scarlet Gibson'

Clematis trailing through the border

Clematis allowed to grow horizontally at ground level can provide a wonderful splash of colour in the summer border. Unless you want the bed to be totally covered by the clematis, choose a variety that is not too rampant and select a colour that will enhance other plants in the border. The herbaceous, non-clinging varieties make ideal companions for small shrubs and perennial plants.

Another method is to train some clematis stems up a fence or tripod, allowing other stems to trail through the border. Two clematis together, such as a large hybrid and small viticella, given their own space in the border or allowed to tumble over low-growing shrubs will provide a mass of colour for many weeks.

Clematis 'Huldine' brightens this bed of pink cranesbill geraniums

'Lady Northcliffe' and pink cranesbill geraniums

The deep yellow stamens of herbaceous *Clematis* 'Durandii' complement the yellow hermerocallis (day lily) in this summer border

Clematis in containers

With a little forward planning, pots and containers on the patio or terrace can be ablaze with colour all summer long, and by incorporating clematis into the plan, colour can be enjoyed at eye level and above. It is essential to plant clematis in large containers and provide the right conditions for their cultivation, so do read the relevant section in Chapter 2 before embarking upon the project.

If your patio adjoins the house and there is no opportunity to create a bed, a large wooden container measuring approximately 65 x 65cm (25½ x 25½in) and 45cm (18in) deep, can contain enough growing medium to support a collection of plants that will provide interest throughout the seasons. Place the container against the house wall on to which trellis has been fixed and prepare it for planting as recommended. The plans shown overleaf show two ways in which a large container can be planted, but there are many other ways you can create your own special mini garden.

PLANTING PLAN BASED ON A PALE PINK ROSE

'Miss Bateman', a stunning clematis for a container

You will need:

1 container, 60 x 56 x 45cm (24 x 22 x 18in)

1 climbing rose 'New Dawn'. Clusters of double, fragrant, pale pearl-pink flowers from summer to autumn. 3m (10ft)

1 *Clematis* 'Miss Bateman'. Single, large white flowers with deep pink anthers. Flowers May–June, occasionally in September. 2m (6½ft)

1 *C. viticella* 'Royal Velours'. Rich, purple-red with deep red anthers. Velvety blooms from July–September. 3m (10ft)

6 pink lillies

3 white busy Lizzies

2 pink verbena

In the autumn, remove the busy Lizzies and the verbena, and replace them with standard and dwarf pink and white tulips for spring

C. viticella 'Royal Velours' has a velvety sheen

Rosa 'New Dawn', one of the most popular climbers

PLANTING PLAN BASED ON WINTER-FLOWERING JASMINE

Autumn sun enhances the purple hue of C. 'Multi Blue'

C. viticella 'Minuet' is an ideal choice for a container

This planting plan is predominately yellow and blue for winter and spring, and pink, blue and silver for summer

You will need:

1 container, 60 x 56 x 45cm (24 x 22 x 18in)

1 *Jasminum nudiflorum*. Deciduous climber. Yellow flowers in winter before leaves are formed in spring

1 *Clematis* 'Multi Blue'. A very interesting plant; the blue flowers, with silver reverse, are double, semi-double and single, sometimes all blooming together. Flowers May–June and September. 2.5m (8ft)

1 *Clematis* 'Minuet'. From the *viticella* family. Cream sepals edged with rosy-mauve

Underplant with:

2 *Senecio cineraria* 'Silver Dust'. Grown for its lovely silver leaves to complement the silver reverse of 'Multi Blue'. Pinch out the flower buds as the yellow is strident and the flowers insignificant

Fill in with blue pansies and pink verbena to trail over the edges

In autumn, remove the pansies and verbena and fill with yellow tulips, hyacinths and blue scilla for the spring

5

AUTUMN GLORY

SEPTEMBER arrives, heralded by a slight nip in the air and shorter daylight hours. Summer bedding plants begin to look tired, but once they are cleared away, a well-planned autumn garden can be full of warm and vibrant colour. Trees and shrubs chosen for their autumnal display; chrysanthemum; dahlias; Michaelmas daisies; the rich, glowing colours of sedum loved by butterflies; clumps of autumn crocus and cyclamen – all are perfectly complemented by late-flowering clematis.

As a bonus, some of the early-flowering clematis hybrids often have a second burst from late summer into autumn and the *viticella* family seems to bloom interminably.

The abundant blooms of *viticella* 'Royal Velours' clothing a tree trunk play a significant role in the overall effect of this early autumn scene at Marwood Gardens, north Devon

For clematis lovers no autumn garden is complete without the yellow, nodding bells of an *orientalis* with their fluffy seed heads sparkling in the warm sunlight. Another lovely addition is the deep pink flowers of the tulip-shaped *texensis* group.

The seasons merge in a very subtle way with much depending upon the climatic conditions of the region and general weather patterns. Sometimes a September day can be warmer than one in mid-summer and a long, warm autumn, especially if accompanied by drying winds, can lead to an extended season for the watering can or hose.

When we emerge in the morning, it is the dew that indicates that the nights have started getting cooler. The water vapour in the air condenses, leaving jewel-like droplets glistening in the early morning sun.

C. viticella 'Royal Velours' bathed in early morning dew

145

Fortunately, most dormant clematis survive even the coldest of winters with their roots snug under the ground and their stems protected by a strong, woody coating. A thick mulch of compost or well-rotted manure around established clematis applied at the end of October will not only help to protect roots, but will enable worms and winter rain to draw the mulch down to feed the soil in readiness for next spring's root growth. Keep the mulch away from the clematis stems to prevent them from rotting.

October is also a good month for planting clematis, because the ground is still warm and plants will have a chance to become established and produce flowers the following year.

If the lower leaves of clematis turn brown and die, they can be removed. However, it is often pests and diseases that are the biggest cause of disfigured clematis. The war against them should continue if clematis are to be enjoyed at their best. Mildew can often ruin an otherwise beautiful plant; this disease is usually caused by dryness around the root system and lack of air circulating around the growth. Preventative measures are the best answer. There is more about the control of pests and diseases and guidance on planting and supporting clematis in Chapter 2.

As autumn progresses into winter and the air temperature drops to freezing, water vapour turns to frost. Only the hardy, winter-flowering *cirrhosa* will withstand such cold conditions and then only for very short periods. However, if you can find a warm, sheltered wall, or a conservatory, you can enjoy the cream bells and fine, feathery foliage of *cirrhosa* all winter long. There is even a variety called 'Jingle Bells' that can reputedly be in full flower on Christmas day.

It is possible to have clematis in flower every month of the year and surely there is no other group of plants that can bring such diversity, colour and charm to the garden.

AUTUMN PARTNERSHIPS

During late summer and early autumn, the large clematis that bloomed in May and June often produce a second flush of flowers, especially if they receive a light pruning after their first flowering and are well fed and watered. Perhaps because they expend so much energy the first time around, the second blooms of the double-flowered varieties are usually single. Many *viticella* types also continue to produce an abundance of flowers, enabling some of the summer partnerships to be enjoyed during September.

Late, large-flowered hybrids usually continue to produce their splendid blooms in September, none more prolifically and reliably than 'Huldine' which looks just as attractive

C. 'Huldine' flowers for a long season

when viewed from the rear, because its sepals are flushed and veined with pink.

When planning clematis for the autumn garden, the glowing colours of the season are best expressed with the warm golden-yellow of the *orientalis* family and the earthy pink of *texensis*. There are many varieties in both groups that look glorious when grown through climbers, roses, shrubs and trees.

Clematis and roses

Modern roses, like the early, large clematis cultivars, often produce a second flush during late summer and early autumn. In favourable conditions both clematis and roses can give a good show into early winter.

Most of the clematis early hybrids have a rest for a few weeks following their main burst

C. 'Marie Boisselot' makes a perfect companion for climbing rose 'Compassion'

Climbing rose 'Compassion' with seed heads of 'Marie Boisselot'

in May and June, but there are some that flower continuously throughout summer and early autumn. During the autumn of 1997, 'Marie Boisselot' and the climbing rose 'Compassion' were planted together on a warm, south-eastern wall of the author's Devon home. They commenced blooming the following summer and continued virtually non-stop into December when the last pink rose bud finally refused to open and the white clematis sepals turned brown in the cooler, damp conditions. They didn't quite make it into the New Year.

'New Dawn' is another climbing rose that blooms on into autumn. The pale, pearly-pink,

There are delicate pink veins on the rear of C. 'Huldine'

Climbing rose 'New Dawn' and late species *triternata*, soft pink partners for early autumn

The dainty, warm and very beautiful *Clematis* 'Princess Diana' is one of the most attractive of the *texensis* family and a fitting tribute

sweetly scented flowers will tolerate partial shade and it looks particularly lovely when grown on a pillar. In the summer chapter, 'New Dawn' was shown partnered with clematis 'Sealand Gem' on a simple wooden screen constructed to hide a storage tank. This gardener had the foresight to plant both 'Sealand Gem' and late species *triternata* with the rose and now enjoys a summer and early autumn theme of soft pink.

There are a number of shrub roses that flower in September and it is not difficult to select lovely partnerships. For example, *Rosa* 'Boule de Neige', an old-fashioned shrub rose, grows to 1.5m (5ft) and has fully double white flowers that emit a heady perfume. Partner it with deep pink *texensis* 'Princess Diana' and the 'Princess' will draw out the slightly pink tone of this charming white rose. *Texensis* varieties look especially lovely when they are

C. texensis 'Ladybird Johnson' and *Rosa* 'Santa Catalina' provide a warm, pink glow

growing through pink roses. Additionally, *Rosa* 'Graham Thomas', a shrub rose with rather lax, arching branches and a mass of golden-yellow, double blooms provides the perfect foil for *orientalis* 'Orange Peel'.

Not all of the roses last into the autumn and those that are without flowers can look quite bare and uninteresting, but not when they are clothed in late-flowering clematis.

Britain's wild clematis, *vitalba*, displays a mass of fluffy heads in autumn, making quite a impressive sight in hedgerows and the edges of woodland as it partners the scarlet hips of the wild dog rose. Cultivated roses and clematis can be grown together in the garden to create equally pleasing and even more

C. viticella 'Etoile Violette' provides a mass of colour on this rose-clad pillar after the rose blooms have finished

C. orientalis 'Orange Peel' and shrub rose 'Graham Thomas' provide a golden autumn glow when grown together

Glossy camellia leaves and the nodding bells of *orientalis* glow in the autumn sunlight

impressive hip and seed head partnerships. There are varieties of *rugosa* and *moyesii* shrub roses that can play host to clematis and provide three glorious seasons of colour. When coupled with *macropetala* or *alpina*, the dainty clematis flowers adorn the rose in spring before the summer show of vibrantly coloured rose blooms. The silvery clematis seed heads and large, red rose hips are the partnership's final display throughout the autumn.

Shrubs and climbers

When the blooms of spring shrubs are just a memory and the flowers of summer varieties are fading away, clematis can bring new life to autumn. The glossy leaves of camellia and escallonia serve as a lovely background for clematis of the *orientalis* family.

Rhododendrons and azaleas that appeared so spectacular in spring now take on an

C. alpina 'Frances Rivis', with its fluffy heads, and orange rose hips provide some autumn beauty

autumn tint to their leaves and provide a perfect setting for the soft pink tones of a *texensis* or the golden sheen of *orientalis*.

There are a few late-summer flowering shrubs whose blooms continue into autumn and who can form interesting partnerships with clematis. Abelia is a graceful shrub which will slowly reach 2m (6½ft), especially if protected by a sunny wall and planted in free-draining soil. *A. grandiflora* bears white flowers; the pink flush will be complemented by a deep-pink *texensis*. Together they will bloom through mid-summer and early autumn.

Indigofera heterantha also needs a sheltered sunny spot and free-draining soil. The arching branches are bare of leaves until May or even June. The purple-pink, pea-like flower is formed in mid-summer. If this slightly delicate plant is damaged by frost, simply cut all of the stems down to ground level in spring and

Escallonia 'Iveyi' and *C. orientalis* 'Bill Mackenzie' put on an eye-catching autumn show

Rhododendron 'Sesterianum', shown here bursting into spring flower, plays host to *C. texensis* 'Glauca Akebioides' which will flower later in the year

Abelia x grandiflora, an autumn-flowering shrub

new shoots will soon appear. *Texensis* 'Gravetye Beauty' with its upward-facing, tulip-shaped flowers makes a colourful partner for indigofera from July right through until the end of September.

The evergreen family of hebe originates from New Zealand and some of the more popular varieties are quite hardy. They are easy to grow on any well-drained soil and do not require pruning. *H.* 'Midsummer Beauty' has lavender-coloured flowers that will complement a deep-purple *viticella* such as 'Elvan' or 'Etoile Violette'.

Viticella 'Polish Spirit' will often flower well into October, making it a perfect choice for the autumn garden. The deep-purple blooms are shown to full advantage against the golden leaves of a shrub or climber.

C. texensis 'Glauca Akebioides' steals the autumn show

C. 'Polish Spirit' weaving through *wisteria*

C. 'Gravetye Beauty' and *Indigofera heterantha*

PLANTING PLAN FOR A RAISED CORNER BED

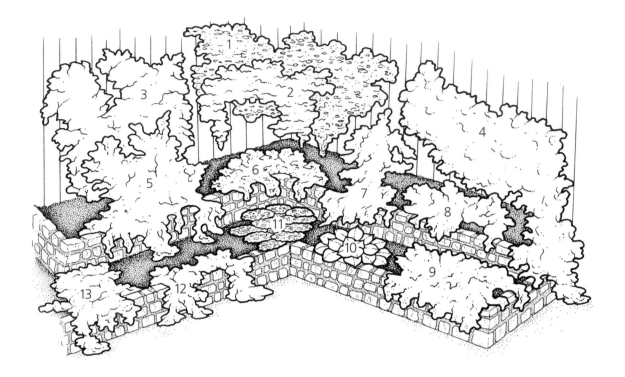

Boundary fences or walls can be used to good effect by building raised beds around a corner. This planting plan is aimed at warm and vibrant autumn colours with a splash of colour for spring. The beds will need to be built to a minimum depth of 45cm (18in). If it is adjacent to a fence, the back of the enclosure will need to be of brick or blocks or the weight of the soil will make the fence unstable and dampness will rot the wood.

Whilst empty, dig the base soil and firm it by treading. Cover with an 8cm (3in) layer of coarse peat. Fill the enclosures with a mixture of 4 parts fibrous acid (lime-free) loam, 1 part sphagnum peat and 1 part coarse sand (lime-free). When the planting is complete, cover the surface with 2.5cm (1in) of sphagnum peat. The mulch will need to be topped up annually.

For the gardener with alkaline soil, raised beds provide a wonderful opportunity to grow lime-hating plants. However, if you do not want to go to the expense of filling the beds with an acid planting medium, replace the rhododendrons and cassiope with alkaline-tolerant plants such as *Berberis thunbergii atropurpurea* 'Nana', *Hebe pinguifolia* 'Pagei' and *Hebe* 'Carl Teschner'.

Clematis is happy either to climb or tumble and here they have the chance to do both. You may have to trim and train more than usual throughout the growing season or they will become entangled in one another and other plants as they tumble down over the beds. Parthenocissus (Virginia creeper) is very rampant and it is advisable to plant it further along the fence or wall and let it grow back towards the corner bed as this will make it easier to control.

PLANTING PLAN FOR A RAISED CORNER BED

Solanum jasminoides and C. 'Henryii' flower from summer to autumn

C. texensis 'Duchess of Albany' brightens an autumn bed

Persicaria vacciniifolia tumbles from a raised bed

1 *Solanum jasminoides* 'Album'. An evergreen or semi-evergreen climber with fragrant white flowers from summer to autumn, followed by ovoid black fruits. This tender climber will need winter protection

2 *Clematis* 'Henryi'. Large, creamy white sepals offset by chocolate-brown anthers. Can reach 3m (10ft) but will not mind being kept in check. A bright, glowing partnership with *Solanum* from summer–autumn

3 *Clematis rehderiana*. Panicles of tubular, pale yellow flowers. Gentle, cowslip-like perfume. Mid-summer to late autumn. Will grow 2–3m (6½–10ft)

4 *Parthenocissus henryana*. White-veined green leaves which turn bright red in autumn. 10m (33ft) spread, but not nearly as rampant as some of the Virginia creepers. Will need to be kept in check, however, especially in a small garden. Prune back before it becomes entangled in the clematis

5 *Clematis texensis* 'Duchess of Albany'. Tulip-shaped, deep pink flowers bloom between mid-summer and autumn

6 *Rhododendron* 'Addy Wery'. Evergreen azalea with an abundance of funnel-shaped vermilion-red flowers in spring

7 *Clematis viticella* 'Tentel'. Dark, rosy-pink flowers with frilled edges bloom between mid-summer and autumn

8 *Rhododendron* 'Kure-no-yuki'. Evergreen. White flowers in spring. 1m (3¼ft)

9 *Persicaria vacciniiflora*. Creeping, semi-evergreen perennial; glossy mid-green leaves which turn red in autumn. Bell-shaped, deep pink flowers from summer to autumn

10 *Hosta* 'Hadspen Blue'. Bold, heart-shaped, blue-grey leaves

11 *Sedum spectabile* 'Brilliant'. The 'ice plant' loved by bees. Bright pink flowers. Summer to early autumn

12 *Diascia* 'Salmon Supreme'. Mat-forming perennial with heart-shaped leaves and pale apricot flowers. Summer to autumn

13 *Cassiope lycopodioides*. Evergreen, mat-forming shrub. Tubular, white, short-stemmed flowers. Late spring

▲ *Jasminum officinale* 'Aureum' provides a golden backcloth for *C. viticella* 'Polish Spirit'

◀ *C. viticella* 'Polish Spirit', grown horizontally to complement *Aster divaricatus*

▼ Abutilon

The deep pink of the *texensis* group also looks effective when they tumble over variegated shrubs. Grown horizontally through the border they make ideal partners for dahlia and other autumn perennials.

'Bill Mackenzie' is one of the finest varieties of the *orientalis* group. The golden bells are larger than type and some of the flowers die, leaving their silvery seed heads, while new flowers are formed at the same time, creating a mass of gold and silver to shimmer in the autumn sunlight.

'Bill Mackenzie' is quite a rampant grower and if paired with other climbers or wall shrubs will need a large wall or fence for support. Abutilon is a tender shrub but some varieties, such as 'Kentish Belle' or 'Milleri' will withstand some frost if planted against a warm wall. Abutilon's flowers and 'Bill's' seed heads make a glorious pairing as they shimmer in the autumn sun.

'Bill Mackenzie' has been known to flower in May if left unpruned and is therefore an ideal candidate for partial pruning. This works

C. texensis 'Gravetye Beauty' complements a bold red and white dahlia

C. orientalis 'Bill Mackenzie' and *viticella* 'Purpurea Plena Elegans' cover a summerhouse at RHS Rosemoor garden in north Devon

157

'Bill Mackenzie' enjoys this south-facing wall with *Tropaeolum speciosum*, the Chilean flame creeper

well if it is to be grown through an apple, pear or plum tree, because the branches will be clothed in beautiful flowers for many weeks and the seed heads will add interest during the winter months.

Another good late-flowering climber is *Tropaeolum speciosum*. A native of Chile, the 'flame creeper' requires moist soil and, like clematis, flourishes when its roots are in the shade and its head is in the sunshine. The spectacular flame-red flowers in summer and early autumn are followed by blue fruits with red collars. Plant it against a warm, south-facing wall. It may be cut back in severe weather.

Seed heads

As the sepals of clematis die and fall, the plant sets its seed in the next step towards reproduction. Clematis seeds are very cleverly formed. Attached to each one is a little tail

'Bill Mackenzie' and a late-flowering honeysuckle can easily reach the roof when grown on a house wall

C. 'Asao' in late autumn. The sepals have died and the seed heads are forming

The attractive seed heads of 'Bill McKenzie' glisten in the autumn sunlight

which helps the seed to become airborne in the wind and then, once it has landed, anchors the seed to the earth. These little tails are what makes clematis seed heads so attractive, and each species and cultivar has its own unique design. Flower arrangers love to use the more intricately formed examples as part of their autumn displays. They can also be a very attractive garden feature as they glow in the autumn sunlight or capture the morning dew. Later they glisten with a coating of frost.

It is not only the *orientalis* family that bears attractive seed heads. Spring-flowering *macropetala* and *alpina* are especially lovely;

'Nelly Moser' seed head clothed in autumn dew

The beautifully formed seed head of *macropetala*

their silver twirls turn into fluff as the seasons progress and they prepare to leave the parent plant and launch into the unknown. Some of the large-flowered hybrids produce intricate shapes that look as if they have been woven; these are especially sought after by flower arrangers.

The berries of cotoneaster and pyrancantha look almost as good as rose hips alongside clematis seed heads and the glossy, evergreen leaves of camellia once again prove to be the perfect setting, this time for the silver heads of *orientalis*. There are many combinations to choose from.

Late species clematis

There are many small, late species clematis that flower until late September. They are not so readily available from garden centres, so you may have to treat yourself to a visit to a specialist clematis nursery to find them. If there

Glossy camellia leaves once again provide a lovely backcloth, this time for the sparkling seed heads of *C. orientalis*

The last, lingering flower of this dainty herbaceous clematis of the *integrifolia* family will soon form into another delightful seed head

is not one nearby, a catalogue and a mail-order service is usually available.

If you refer to the list of late, small-flowered clematis that begins on page 62, you will see there are a quite a number of these little beauties available in a range of colours, shapes and sizes to grow as specimen features or in partnership with autumn shrubs.

C. potanini is a vigorous grower climbing to 5m (16½ft), tolerant of most aspects. The mass of small, white, spreading flowers with their crown of yellow anthers makes a magnificent display against a large evergreen shrub such as *Ceanothus impressus* 'Pugets Blue'. This 3m (10ft) shrub with intense blue flowers will make an impressive show from mid- to late spring, leaving its verdant green leaves for the display of *potanini* later.

C. flammula has an unusual almond scent and a mass of small, white, star-shaped flowers from July to October. It looks lovely when grown as a specimen plant or through an open shrub such as *Hamamelis x intermedia* 'Diane' whose leaves turn yellow and red in autumn and whose spidery, deep-red flowers appear on the bare branches from mid- to late winter.

C. rehderiana is another late species that should not be missed. Provide a sunny position to enjoy its large panicles of cowslip-like flowers with a perfume to match.

Days shorten and grow colder as autumn turns to winter. Hardy gardeners tie in their climbers against the winter winds, remove diseased and decaying leaves to prevent soil contamination and watch in amazement as the evergreen clematis, *cirrhosa*, sheltered against a warm house wall, opens its cream bells in defiance of the winter chill. Clematis belonging to the *cirrhosa* group are vigorous growers if given the right location and conditions. In southern counties of Britain and warm climate zones they will often survive the winter and produce a mass of beautiful flowers. In less temperate zones, grow them in a large container placed in

Clematis rehderiana looks and smells like cowslips

a frost-free, well-lit porch or conservatory.

Now is the time for planning and to reflect on the garden as it has been during the past seasons, and to seek new ideas for clematis companions for the coming year. With so many varieties available and so many different pairings to choose from, you can create your own unique little haven of colour for virtually every month of the year.

GLOSSARY

Acid Soil with a pH value below 7

Alkaline Soil with a pH value above 7

Annual A plant that completes its life cycle in one growing season, usually referring to summer bedding plants

Anther The upper part of the stamen that contains the pollen

Bed Area of ground, usually cultivated, in which plants are grown

Berry The fruit of plants made up of soft flesh surrounding seeds

Bisexual Refers to a plant with both male and female reproductive organs

Bract A modified leaf-like structure, which can sometimes appear petal-like that grows between the leaf and stem

Calyx Collective name for the outer whorl of sepals

Clematis 'Lasurstern', showing stamens

Chlorosis A loss of chlorophyll (a green pigment that absorbs energy from sunlight) caused by a mineral deficiency, poor light levels or disease

Corolla Collective name for petals

Cultivar A plant that is artificially raised or selected and its characteristics can be maintained by propagation

Deciduous A plant that sheds its leaves annually at the end of its growing season

Ericaceous A plant belonging to the Ericaceae family. Describes potting compost with a pH of 6.5 or less in which acid loving plants can be grown

Evergreen A plant that retains its leaves for more than one growing season

Foliar feed A diluted solution of fertilizer, normally sprayed onto plants, which then absorbs the nutrients through its leaves

Frost hardy A plant that is able to withstand temperatures down to −5°C (23°F)

Friable soil Soil that is easily broken up, crumbly

Frost tender Temperatures below 5°C (41°F) may cause damage

Fully hardy A plant that is able to withstand temperatures down to −15°C (5°F)

Fungicide An agent, usually a chemical, that destroys or helps to prevent fungal disease.

Fungus A mould or mushroom that survives by absorbing nutrients and organic material from its surroundings

Genus A family or plant species that share a wide range of characteristics

Ground frost When the temperature at soil level, or just below the surface, falls to 0°C (32°F)

Humus Organic material that has slowly decomposed. Also refers to rotted garden compost or leaf mould, which can be dug into the soil to improve texture

Hybrid Naturally or artificially produced offspring of at least two different varieties of plants. They can be similar to their parents or bear no resemblance at all. Successful hybridization combines the best qualities of each parent plant

Internode The part of a stem between two nodes (leaf joints)

Layering A method of propagation where the stem of a plant is pegged down into the soil to encourage rooting whilst it is still attached to the parent plant

Loam Earth that usually contains equal parts of sand, clay and silt, producing a highly fertile, well drained, humus rich soil

Node A joint at the stem of a plant, which is sometimes swollen, from which leaf buds and shoots are formed

Ovoid Egg-shaped with the broader end at the base

Perennial A plant that lives for more than two growing seasons

Petal The corolla of a flower, really a modified leaf, that is brightly coloured to attract insects

PH A measure of acidity or alkalinity. A wide range of plants prefer neutral or slightly acid soil of pH 5.5 to 7.5

Pinch out Sometimes referred to as stop. To remove soft growing points to encourage the bushy growth of side shoots

Pistil The female reproductive organ of a plant, consisting of one or several carpels which may be joined

Pollen grains of the anthers containing the male element necessary for fertilisation

Pollination The transfer of pollen to the stigma. Insects and animals perform this operation but it can be done by hand

Recurving Curving or bending back or down

Clematis 'Charissima'

Reflexed Arched or bent back upon itself

Sepal Part of the calyx. Sepals are often green and form as a protective shield for the petals, they fold back as the buds open. Sometimes the sepals are colourful and petal-like and the flower is formed by a whorl of sepals alone

Species A group of plants where the flowers and foliage are of the plants original habit and these characteristics differentiate them from another group

Stamen Male part of a flower

Systemic Mostly used to describe a type of insecticide which is absorbed by the plant, making it toxic to pests whilst preserving the health of the plant

Tendril On climbing plants, a coiling leaflet or shoot, used to attach itself to a support.

Tepal The petals and sepals of a flower, which often whorl around together, making it difficult to separate them

Whorl Circular arrangement of leaves, petals, sepals, tepals or shoots, arising from a single point

ABOUT THE AUTHOR

MARIGOLD BADCOCK discovered the joy of gardening when she and her husband Edward renovated the neglected garden of their first home; the design was to change many times during their twenty-year stay.

Gardening had to be fitted in with a busy working and family life. After spending many years in a commercial sales environment, Marigold embarked upon a new career providing day services for adults with a learning disability, which proved to be both emotionally rewarding and personally stimulating.

Two more house moves enabled Marigold to experiment with her love of garden design and combination planting. She also became more absorbed in her photographic hobby and gained her Licentiateship to the Royal Photographic Society in 1992.

Now retired and living in the heart of the north Devon countryside, Marigold shares her love of gardening and photography in this her first book.

USEFUL ADDRESSES

Contact your national clematis society for further information and a list of local suppliers.

British Clematis Society
2 Gatley Avenue
West Ewell
Surrey KT19 9NG
Tel. 01276 476387

American Clematis Society
c/o Edith Malek
P.O. Box 17085
Irvine,

CA 92623-7085
Tel. 949-224-9885
Email: edith@clematis.org

International Clematis Society
3 Cuthberts Close
Goffs Oak
Hertfordshire EN7 5RB
Tel: 01953 850407
Email: http://www.garden
web.com/directory/icls/

Canadian membership:
Llyn Strelau
1643 Altadore Avenue

S.W.
Calgary
Alberta T2T 2P8
Email: clematis@dial.
pipex.com

USA membership:
Victoria Mattthews
Denver Botanic Gardens
909 York Street
Denver CO 80206-3799

INDEX

Abelia 151, 152
Abutilon 118, 156, 157
Acacia (mimosa) 67, 92–3
Actinidia kolomikta 110–11
Anemone blanda 107
aphids 83
arbours 73–5
Asarum europaeum 99
Ascochyta clemcidina 83
autumn 144–61
azaleas 108, 134, 150–1

backcloth to a border 132–3
Berberis thunbergii atropurpurea 95
Betula (silver birch) 90, 91
border
    backcloth to 132–3
    clematis trailing through 140

Camassia leichtlinii 107
Camellia 95–6, 134, 150, 160
Campanula 60, 125
Cassiope lycopodioides 155
Ceanothus 111–12
Ceanothus impressus 160
Cedrus deodara 97
Cestrum 112–13
Chaenomeles japonica 127–8
Chamaecyparis obtusa 97
Choisya ternata 96

choosing clematis 67–8, 90
Cistus x corbarienses 125
Clematis
    'Abundance' 43
    'Akaishi' 24
    'Alabast' 24
    'Alba' (*integrifolia*) 53
    'Alba' (*montana*) 21
    'Alba Luxurians' 43, 122
    'Alba Plena' 46, 47
    'Albina Plena' 18
    'Alexander' 21
    'Alice Fisk' 24
    'Aljonushka' 53
    'Allanah' 24
    alpina 14–16, 90, 94–100, 159–60
    'Ametistina' 15
    'Amy' 53
    'Andromeda' 24
    'Anna' 24
    'Anna Louise' 24
    'Annabel' 24
    'Annemieke' 62
    apilifolia 62
    'Apple Blossom' 12
    'Arabella' 54, 66
    'Arctic Queen' 24, 106, 107, 119
    armandii 10, 12, 90, 91–2
    'Aromatica' 54
    'Asagasumi' 24
    'Asao' 24, 110, 111, 159
    'Ascotiensis' 47
    'Aureolin' 57
    'Ballet Skirt' 18
    'Barbara Dibley' 25
    'Barbara Jackman' 25
    'Beauty of Richmond' 25
    'Beauty of Worcester' 25
    'Bees Jubilee' 25
    'Bella' 47
    'Belle Nantaise' 25, 114–15
    'Belle of Woking' 25
    'Bessie Watkinson' 25
    'Betina' 15

    'Betty Corning' 43
    'Betty Risdon' 26
    'Bill Mackenzie' 56, 57, 151, 157–8, 159
    'Black Madonna' 26
    'Black Prince' 43, 47
    'Black Prince' (*viticella*) 43
    'Blue Angel' (Blekitny Aniol) 47
    'Blue Belle' 43
    'Blue Bird' 18
    'Blue Dancer' 15
    'Blue Gem' 26
    'Blue Ravine' 26
    'Bluebird' 15
    'Blush Queen' 15
    'Bowl of Beauty' 12
    'Bracebridge Star' 26
    brachyura 54
    'Broughton Star' 21
    'Brunette' 15
    buchananiana 62
    'Burford Bell' 62
    'Burford Variety' 57
    'Burford White' 15
    'Calycina' 11
    campaniflora 62
    'Campanile' 54
    'Candy Stripe' 26
    'Capitaine Thuilleaux' 26
    'Cardinal Wyszynski' 47
    'Carnaby' 26, 137
    'Carnival Queen' 26
    'Caroline' 4, 27, 104, 121
    categories 9
    'Chalcedony' 27
    'Charissima' 26, 27
    'Chili' (formerly 'Harry Smith') 18
    chinensis 63
    chrysocoma 21
    'Cicciolina' 43
    cirrhosa 10–12, 90, 91, 146, 161; var. *balaerica* 11
    'Colette Deville' 27
    'Columbine' 15
    'Comtesse de Bouchard' 47, 137

    connata 63
    'Constance' 15
    'Corona' 26, 27, 113
    'Cote d'Azur' 54
    'Countess of Lovelace' 27
    'Crepuscule' 54
    'Crimson King' 27
    crispa 63
    crispa hybrid (not yet named) 63
    'C.W. Dowman' 27
    'Cyanea' 15
    'Cylindrica' 63
    'Daniel Deronda' 27
    'Dawn' 27
    'Debutante' 27
    'Denny's Double' 27
    'Directeur André Devillers' 27
    'Doctor Ruppel' 27, 112
    'Dorothy Tolver' 27
    'Dorothy Walton' 27, 47
    'Duchess of Albany' 60, 155
    'Duchess of Edinburgh' 28
    'Duchess of Sutherland' 28
    'Durandii' 54, 55, 123, 125, 141
    'Early Sensation' 11, 94
    'Edith' 28
    'Edomurasaki' 28, 140
    'Edouard Desfossé' 28
    'Edward Pritchard' 54
    'Elizabeth' 20, 21
    'Elsa Späth' 28, 134
    'Elvan' 43, 152

Clematis, continued
  'Empress of India' 28
  'Entel' 43
  eriostemon
    'Hendersonii' 53,
    104, 105
  'Ernest Markham' 28,
  99, 115
  'Etoile de Malicorne'
  28
  'Etoile de Paris' 29
  'Etoile Rose' 60
  'Etoile Violette' 43,
  139, 149, 152
  'Fair Rosamond' 29
  'Fairy Queen' 29
  'Fireworks' 29
  flammula 62, 63, 106,
  161
  'Floriala' 18
  florida 46, 47
  'Floris V' 53
  forsteri 13, 93–4
  'Foxtrot' 44
  'Foxy' 15
  'Fragrant Spring' 21
  'Frances Rivis' 15, 16,
  95, 98, 100, 151
  'Frankie' 15, 99
  'Freckles' 11
  'Freda' 21
  'Fujimusume' 29
  fusca 63
  fusca violacea 63
  'Gabrielle' 29
  'General Sikorski' 29
  'Gillian Blades' 29, 99,
  108
  'Gipsy Queen' 47, 48,
  133
  'Gladys Picard' 30
  'Glauca Akebioides'
  58, 152, 153
  'Glynderek' 30
  'Golden Harvest' 57
  'Gothenburg' 21
  gouriana 63
  'Grace' 63
  'Grandiflora' 21, 22

grata 63
'Gravetye Beauty' 60,
  61, 152, 153, 157
'Gravetye Variety' 57
'Guernsey Cream' 30,
  99, 105
'Guiding Star' 48
'Hagley Hybrid' 5, 48,
  128
'Haku Ookan' 30
'Hanaguruma' 30
'Helen Cropper' 30
'Helios' 57
'Helsingborg' 15
'Henryi' 30, 31, 155
heracleifolia 52
heracleifolia davidiana
  53
'Herbert Johnson' 30
'H. F. Young' 30
'Hikarugenji' 30
hilariae 63
hirsutissima var. *scottii*
  54
'Horn of Plenty' 30, 31
'Huldine' 48, 120,
  140, 146–7
'Hybrida Sieboldii' 30
'Imperial' 30
indivisa 11, 12, 92
integrifolia 52, 53, 160
intricata (*akebiodes*)
  64
'Ishobel' 30
ispahanica 54
'Ivan Olsen' 31
'Jackmanii' 2, 48, 122,
  132, 139
'Jackmanii Alba' 2,
  129
'Jackmanii Rubra' 130
'Jacqueline du Pré' 15
'Jacqui' 21
'James Mason' 31
'Jan Lindmark' 18
'Jenny Caddick' 48
'Jim Hollis' 31
'Jingle Bells' 11, 146
'Joan Gray' 31
'Joan Picton' 23, 31
'Joe' (*Cartmanii* Joe')
  13, 54
'John Huxtable' 48
'John Paul II' 31
'John Warren' 31
'Josephine TM Johill'
  32, 33
jouiniana 54
jouiniana 'Praecox' 54,
  55, 118

'Kakio' ('Pink
  Champagne') 32
'Kardynal Wysznski'
  32
'Kasugayama' 32
'Kathleen Dunford' 32
'Kathleen Wheeler' 32
'Keith Richardson' 32
'Ken Donson' 32
'Kermesina' 44, 133,
  134
'King Edward VII' 32
'King George V' 32
'Kiri Te Kanawa' 32
kirilowii 64
'Königskind' 32
'Laciniifolia' 58
ladakhiana 64
'Lady Betty Balfour'
  48
'Ladybird Johnson' 60,
  149
'Lady Caroline Nevill'
  32
'Lady Londesborough'
  32
'Lady Northcliffe' 32,
  98, 99, 131, 141
'Lady in Red' 32
'Lagoon' 18
'Lambton Park' 57
lasiandra 64
'Lasurstern' 32, 33
'Lauren' 53
'Lavender Lace' 32
'Lawsoniana' 33
'Lemon Chiffon' 33
'Liberation' 33
ligusticifolia 64
'Lilac Time' 33
'Lilacina' (*montana*)
  21
lilacina floribunda 33,
  34
'Lincoln Star' 33
'Lisboa' 64
'Little Nell' 44
'Lord Nevill' 33
'Louise Rowe' 33

'Lucey' 48
macropetala 17–19,
  69, 90, 94–100,
  125, 159–60
'Madame Baron
  Veillard' 48
'Madame Edouard
  André' 49
'Madame Grangé' 49,
  121
'Madame Julia
  Correvon' 44
'Maidwell Hall' 18
mandshurica 54
'Marcel Moser' 34
'Margaret Hunt' 49,
  111, 136
'Margaret Jones' 21
'Margaret Wood' 34
'Margot Koster' 44,
  45, 73, 117, 127
'Marie Boisselot' 34,
  147
'Marie Louise Jensen'
  34
'Marjorie' 22, 102
'Markham's Pink' 19,
  99
'Marmut' 33
'Marwood x' 35
'Mary Rose' (*viticella*
  'Flore Pleno') 44
'Masquerade' 34, 35
'Maureen' 34
'Mayleen' 22
'Meyeniana' 12
'Miikla' 49
'Minuet' 44, 45, 143
'Miriam Markham' 34
'Miss Bateman' 34,
  105, 142
'Miss Crawshay' 34
montana 1, 20–2, 67,
  90, 101–3
'Monte Cassino' 34,
  49
'Moonlight' 35
'Mrs Bush' 35
'Mrs Cholmondley'
  35, 75
'Mrs G. Jackman' 35
'Mrs George Jackman'
  35
'Mrs Hope' 35
'Mrs James Mason' 35
'Mrs Lundell' 44
'Mrs N. Thompson' 35
'Mrs P. B. Truax' 36
'Mrs Robert Brydon'
  54

Clematis, continued
'Mrs Spencer Castle'
  36
'Multi Blue' 36, 105,
  143
'Myojo' 36
napaulensis 13
'Natacha' 36
'Nelly Moser' 36, 104,
  105–9, 159
'New Dawn' 22
'Nikolaj Rubtzov' 49
'Niobe' 49
'Nunn's Gift' 13
'Odorata' (*alpina*) 15
'Odorata' (*montana*)
  22
'Olgae' 53
'Olimpiada-80' 36
'Orange Peel' 58, 149,
  150
orientalis 56–8, 78,
  145, 147, 150, 160
'Pagoda' 61
'Pamela Jackman' 15
'Pangbourne Pink' 53
'Parasol' 37
'Pastel Blue' 53
'Pastel Pink' 53
patens (Chinese form)
  37
patens (Japanese form)
  37
'Patricia Ann Fretwell'
  37, 38
'Paul Farges' (Summer
  Snow) 64
'Pauline' 15
'Pearl Rose' 19
'Perle d'Azur' 49, 50,
  124, 125
'Perrins Pride' 50
peterae 64
'Petit Faucon' 54
'Peveril' (*montana*) 22
'Peveril' (*recta*) 55
'Peveril Pearl' 37
'Picton's Variety' 22,
  101
pierotii 64
'Pink Fantasy' 50
'Pink Flamingo' 15, 97
'Pink Perfection' 22
pitcheri 64
'Pohjanael' 50
'Polish Spirit' 45, 152,
  153, 156
potanini 64, 160
'Prairie River' 15
'Prince Charles' 50

'Prince Philip' 37, 105
'Princess Diana'
  (formerly 'The
  Princess of Wales')
  61, 148
'Princess of Wales' 37
'Prins Hendrik' 37
'Proteus' 37, 93, 138
'Purple Spider' 19
'Purpurea' 55
'Purpurea Plena
  Elegans' 42, 45,
  123, 126, 157
'Queen Alexandra' 37
'Ramona' 37
recta 52, 55
rehderiana 64, 65,
  155, 161
'Rhapsody' 119
'Richard Pennell' 37
'Rosea' 52, 53
'Rosy O'Grady' 19
'Rosy Pagoda' 16
'Rouge Cardinal' 4,
  50, 51, 129
'Royal Velours' 45,
  142, 145
'Royal Velvet' 37
'Royalty' 37
'Rubens' 22

'Rubra' 45
'Ruby' 16, 97
'Ruby Glow' 37
'Rusalka' 55
'Samantha Denny' 37
'Satsukibare' 37
'Saturn' 38
'Scartho Gem' 38
'Sealand Gem' 38,
  121, 148
'Serenata' 38
serratifolia 64
'Sheriffii' 58
'Sho-un' 38
'Sieboldii' 47
'Signe' 38
'Silver Moon' 38

'Sir Garnet Wolseley'
  39
'Sir Trevor Lawrence'
  61
'Snow Queen' 39, 112
'Snowbird' 19
'Snowdrift' 12
'Soldertalje' 45
songarica 55
'Souvenir de J. L.
  Delbard' 39
'Special Occasion' 6,
  38, 39
'Spoonerii' 22
'Sputnik' 50
stans 55
'Star of India' 50
structure, habit and
  shape 7–9
'Sugar Candy' 39
'Sunset' 39
'Superba' 22
'Sylvia Denny' 39
'Sympathia' 39
'Tage Lundell' 16
'Tango' 45
tangutica 56, 57
'Tapestry' 53
'Tateshina' 39
'Tazuki' 39
'Tentel' 45, 155
terniflora 65
'Teshio' 39
'Tetrarose' 22
texensis 59–61, 145,
  147, 148–9
'The Bride' 39
'The President' 40,
  119, 133
'The Vagabond' 40
thunbergii 65
tibetana 56, 58;
  var. *tenuifolia* 58
'Titania' 40
'Trianon' 40
x triternata ('Rubro-
  marginata') 65, 148
'Twilight' 40
veitchiana 65
'Venosa Violacea' 45,
  118
'Vera' 22
'Vernayi' 58
'Vernayi L & S 13342'
  58
'Veronica's Choice' 40
versicolor 55
'Vicky' 19
'Victoria' 50, 136
'Ville de Lyon' 51,

  104, 117, 122, 133,
  138
'Vino' 41
'Viola' 51
'Violet Charm' 41
'Violet Elizabeth' 41
viorna 65
'Viorna' 61
virginiana 65
vitalba (Old Man's
  Beard) 8, 65, 149
viticella 42–5, 118,
  125, 144, 146
'Vivienne Lawson' 51
'Voluceau' 51
'Vostok' 51
'Vyvyan Pennell' 41,
  120, 132
'Wada's Primrose' 41,
  104
'Walter Pennell' 41
'Warsaw Nike' 51
'Warwickshire Rose'
  22
'W. E. Gladstone' 41
'Western Virgin' 65
'Westerplatte' 51
'Westleton' 19
'White Columbine' 16
'White Lady' 19
'White Moth'
  (*alpina*)16
'White Moth'
  (*macropetala*) 19
'White Swan' 19
'Wilhelmina Tull' 10
'Will Goodwin' 41
'William Kennet' 40,
  41, 120
'Willy' 16
'Wilsonii' 22
'Wisley Cream' 12, 89
'W. S. Callick' 41
'Yvette Houry' 41
clematis wilt 2–3, 5,
  83–4
Clianthus albus 126–7
Clianthus puniceus 126,
  127

climbers 8–9, 90
    autumn 150–8
    summer 125–32
Cobaea scandens 126
colours 104–8, 124–5
conifer companions 97
containers 79–81,
    118–19, 141–3
Coprosma 60
corner bed, raised 154–5
Corokia 108
Cotoneaster 137, 160
cranesbill geraniums 140,
    141
Crocus 107
cultivars 7, 162
Cupressus macrocapa 97
cuttings 85–6
Cytisus 53

Dahlia 157
Daphne laureola 99
Diascia 155
diseases 2–3, 5, 83–4,
    146

early to mid-season
    clematis 23–41
earwigs 82
Elymus magellanicus 125
Erica carnea 99
Erythronium
    californicum 107
Escallonia 57, 138, 139,
    150, 151
Euonymous fortunei 96,
    97
evergreen clematis 10–13
    spring 91–4

feeding 3, 76, 90
fence post support 75, 76
fences 69
free-standing supports
    75–6
frost 146

Galanthus 107
Gentiana 125
ground cover 69–70

Hamamelis x intermedia
    161
Hebe 152
herbaceous clematis 9,
    52–5
Hermerocallis 141
holiday care 78
honeysuckle 130–2
Hosta 155

hoverflies 81
hybrids 7, 163
Hydrangea 108, 109,
    136
Hypericum 136, 137

Ilex 139
Indigofera heterantha
    151–2, 153

Jasminum nudiflorum
    143
Jasminum officinale 156

Kolkwitzia 135

labelling 78
large-flowered clematis
    early 104
    late 46–51
late-flowering clematis
    160–1
    large-flowered 46–51
    small-flowered 62–5
Lathyrus grandiflorus
    118
layering 87, 163
Lonicera (honeysuckle)
    130–2

Magnolia 108, 109
mildew 84, 146
mimosa (*Acacia*) 67,
    92–3

Narcissus 107

Osmanthus
    heterophyllus 107,
    138, 139

Parthenocissus 154, 155
Passiflora 127
pergolas 73–5
Persicaria vacciniiflora
    155
pests 81–3, 146

Phormium cookanium
    106–7
photography 5
Physocarpus 134, 135
Pittosporum 93–4, 139
planning 66
planting 70–1
planting plans 106–7,
    124–5, 142–3, 154–5
plants, as supports 71
Potentilla 140
pruning 3, 76–8, 89–90
Prunus 'Pink Perfection'
    102
Prunus serrula 91
Pyracantha 128, 129,
    160

raised corner bed 154–5
rhododendrons 134,
    150–1, 152, 155
Robinia hispida 113–14
Robinia pseudoacacia
    113
Roscoea cauteloides 125
roses (*Rosa*) 75, 119–25,
    147–50
    'Boule de Neige' 148
    'Canary Bird' 125
    'Chinatown' 125
    'Compassion' 2, 147
    'Dorothy Perkins' 123
    'Françoise Juranville'
       123
    'Graham Thomas' 58,
       149, 150
    'Handel' 119, 122
    'Josephine Bruce' 122
    'Maigold' 124, 125
    'Mme Isaac Pereire' 4,
       121
    'New Dawn' 100, 121,
       142, 147–8
    'Raymond Chenault'
       120
    'Rive D'or' 106, 107
    'Santa Catalina' 149
    'Seagull' 129
    'Silver Jubilee' 119
    'Summer Wine' 129

Salvia 112
Sedum spectabile 155
seedheads 158–60
seeds, growing from
    84–5
Senecio cineraria 143
sepals 7–8, 163
serpentine layering 87
shrub companions 68

autumn 150–8
spring 95–6
summer 133–9
site, choosing 66
slugs 82
snails 82
soil 68
Solanum jasminoides 155
species 7, 163
Spiraea 66
spraying chemicals 81
spring 88–115
stamens 7, 8, 163
summer 116–43
suppliers 67
supports 71–6, 98–100
Syringa vulgaris 135–6

tendrils 8, 163
tepals 8, 163
Thunbergia alata 126
transplanting 79
trees 68–9, 97
    summer 133–9
trellis 71–2
tripods 75, 98
trompe l'oeil trellis 72
Tropaeolum peregrinum
    126
Tropaeolum speciosum
    158

Vinca 22
vine eyes 73
vine weevils 83

walls 69
    wall shrubs for
       summer 125–32
watering 76, 90, 117
Weigela 135
wigwam supports 75–6
wilt 2–3, 5, 83–4
wire grid 73
Wisteria 99–100, 128–30